SELF-PUBLISHER'S
LEGAL
HANDBOOK

The Step-by-Step Guide
to the Legal Issues of Self-Publishing

HELEN SEDWICK

TEN GALLON PRESS

SELF-PUBLISHER'S LEGAL HANDBOOK

The Step-by-Step Guide to the Legal Issues of Self-Publishing

Copyright © 2014 by Helen Sedwick

www.helensedwick.com

www.tengallonpress.com

This Handbook should not be used as a substitute for the advice of competent legal counsel from an attorney admitted or authorized to practice in your jurisdiction. You should never delay seeking legal advice, disregard legal advice, or commence or discontinue any legal action because of information in this Handbook.

Cover Design by Mary Mitchell Design
Interior Layout by Ellie Searl, Publishista®
Author Photograph by Star Shots, Santa Rosa, CA

ISBN 13: 978-0988302150
LCCN: 2014936709

Ten Gallon Press
Santa Rosa, CA

This Handbook is dedicated to every writer with

a story to tell,

a memory to share,

an insight to explore,

and a heart to open.

CONTENTS

INTRODUCTION

Congratulations. You have written a book. You have tackled the challenges of voice, pacing, and structure. More kudos to you if you are self-publishing. You are ready to grapple with copyediting, layout, cover art, and ePub.

As a self-publisher, you face new challenges—legal issues as wide ranging as copyright, defamation, and taxes.

Perhaps you are surprised to discover you are starting a business. You have questions about incorporation and crowdfunding, not to mention hiring freelancers and deducting expenses.

Or you are considering buying a publishing package from a self-publishing service company. You wonder how to distinguish between an honest company and an unscrupulous one. You worry about losing your copyright.

Do you suffer from *contract anxiety?* When you try to read a contract, does the page look like 5,000 words run through a blender?

What about author platforms? How do you find eye-catching images without spending a fortune? How do you write blog posts that are provocative but not defamatory? Does your website need a privacy policy, and what do DMCA, COPPA, and DRM mean anyway?

Dozens of books and websites offer advice about designing covers, editing content, and tweeting effectively, but few will tell you how to protect your Social Security Number or spot a scam. Online advice is often wrong, outdated, or incomprehensible. Who has the patience to sort through such clutter? How do you tell useful insight from utter nonsense?

When I self-published my historical novel, *Coyote Winds*, I found no legal guide for self-publishing writers. That needed to change.

I am a business lawyer with 30 years of experience assisting clients in setting up and running their businesses, legally and successfully. My clients include entrepreneurs such as winery owners, green toy makers, software engineers, and writers. I do not go to court, and no one is ever going to produce a movie about the exciting life of a business attorney. But I get a great deal of satisfaction by keeping my clients out of trouble, so they can focus on their businesses, their creative projects, and their lives.

I wrote this book to help other writers self-publish and promote their work while minimizing legal risks and errors.

Writing and publishing a book is a significant investment in both time and money. It is tough enough to make money in a business where fewer than five percent of books sell over 1,000 copies. You don't want to lose that money (or sleep) by hiring the wrong self-publishing service company or getting sued for copyright infringement.

Many chapters in this book will also help a traditionally published writer who is blogging, tweeting, and creating content for Internet distribution.

The goal of this book is to show you how to:

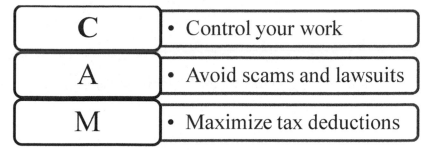

C	• Control your work
A	• Avoid scams and lawsuits
M	• Maximize tax deductions

Control: If you are serious about building your self-publishing business and protecting your rights, then you want to control all components of your work: the copyright, ISBNs, retail pricing, discount rate, distribution channels, and promotions. *Self-Publisher's Legal Handbook* provides the tools for maintaining this control.

Avoid: No one wants to lose money in a scam, buy worthless services, pay unnecessary taxes, or get sued for infringement, defamation, or invasion of privacy. This Handbook will educate you on how to reduce these risks.

Maximize: Your expenses will exceed your revenues, at least at first. I will advise you on how to improve your chances of deducting these expenses from non-book-related income.

Remember this acronym: CAM (control, avoid, maximize). I refer to it often.

Like most business attorneys, I blend legal and business advice. The most cautious legal advice is useless if it makes no business sense. But an aggressive business strategy that crosses the legal line is just as useless and much more damaging. Even if you are writing a book on how to rob a bank or hack the Pentagon, readers expect you to deal with them honestly and competently. Lose a reader's trust, and you'll lose that reader.

To make this Handbook user-friendly, I've organized the book into sections:

Starting Out on the Right Foot. Chapter One walks you through the steps of setting up your business, including registering a DBA (doing business as) name and obtaining a tax identification number.

Moving from Manuscript to Book. Chapter Two compares the options of engaging a self-publishing service company (SPSC) to doing it yourself using a print-on-demand (POD) provider. Chapter Three explains the mechanics of hiring designers, editors, and other freelancers.

Getting Rights Right. Chapter Four covers the basics of copyrights, trademarks, fair use, and public domain, including how to find copyright holders. I provide tips on licensing images and music for little or no money.

Avoiding Marketing and Internet Minefields. Chapter Five discusses marketing and distribution choices, including paid reviews and giveaways. It also covers typical scams such as expensive, but meritless, contests. Chapter Six translates the alphabet soup of SPAM, COPPA, and DMCA. The intimidating topics of defamation and invasion of privacy are covered in Chapter Seven.

The Inevitable Taxes. Chapter Eight touches on the mechanics of sales and income tax, including tips on saving money.

Working Well with Others. Chapter Nine explores collaborations. Chapter Ten explains how to find and retain an attorney.

Beyond the Book. Self-publishing is a new business and still evolving. Law is an old business and still evolving. In the last chapter, I invite you to send me your questions and to share your experiences—the foolish, the infuriating, and the successful. Your contributions may end up in the next edition of the *Self-Publisher's Legal Handbook.*

Addendum. I have annotated and explained key portions of the CreateSpace and KDP (Kindle Direct Publishing for e-books) publishing contracts. Once you know what to look for in a contract, the words will form into concepts, and the concepts will grow into understanding. I also include excerpts from a shockingly predatory (and completely real) contract to help you recognize the fine-print traps to avoid.

You don't need to read the chapters sequentially. You could be working on transforming your manuscript into a paperback and e-book while you are setting up your business and designing your website. Copyright and defamation issues are ongoing, and taxes are forever. I reference useful websites throughout the book, and you will find the web addresses for them in the Addendum and on my website, http://helensedwick.com.

A few disclaimers:

- Although I am a lawyer, I am not *your* lawyer. Reading this book does not create an attorney-client relationship between us.

- If you ask an attorney a question, her favorite answer will be "it depends." In giving legal advice, much depends on the particular facts and personalities involved.

- The information in this book is general in nature and may not apply to your specific situation.

- I am not soliciting you to send me legal work. Frankly, my plate and practice are already quite full.

- I am licensed to practice in the State of California only. While much of what I say applies in many states, I do not know the law in all 50 states, much less foreign jurisdictions.

- This Handbook should not be used as a substitute for the advice of a competent attorney admitted or authorized to practice in your jurisdiction. You should never delay seeking legal advice, disregard legal advice, or commence or discontinue any legal action because of information in this Handbook.

- I provide hyperlinks and references to other resources as a convenience to you. My hyperlinks and references are not meant to imply an approval, endorsement, affiliation, sponsorship or other relationship to the linked resource or its operator.

- I will not tell you, *"Don't worry about it. No one (the IRS/ state sales tax authority/ copyright owner) will ever know."* I will lay out the law and the customary practices. I may suggest the path intended to avoid legal landmines. Whether you follow the law is up to you. Some people enjoy the thrill of living near the edge; others have trouble sleeping when they take any risk.

- If you ask, *"Should I put it in writing?"* the answer is *yes*.

- You may want to consult an attorney directly. I explain how to find, interview, and engage an attorney in *Chapter Ten: Attorneys*.

- On a stylistic level, I will avoid the awkward *his or her*. I may say *his*. I may say *her*. I mean both.

- CIRCULAR 230 DISCLAIMER: If and to the extent that this book contains any tax advice, I am required by the Internal Revenue Service's Circular 230 (31 CFR Part 10) to advise you that such tax advice is not a formal legal opinion and was not intended or written to be used by you, and may not be used by you, (i) for the purpose of avoiding tax penalties that might be imposed on you or (ii) for promoting, marketing or recommending to another party any transaction or matter addressed herein.

Finally, I am assuming:

- You will not be hiring employees. If you are successful enough to hire employees, then I congratulate you. You will soon outgrow this book.

- You are ready to spend some money. If you produce an e-book only and are willing to do your own editing, designing, website design, and so forth, then your outlay could be $100. Or you can spend $30,000 on designers, editors, publicists, and advertising. The choice depends on what you can afford and whether you are giving yourself permission to invest—*yes, invest*—in your dream.

My advice: *Go for it*. You have worked a long time on your book, most likely years. Give it the best chance to spread its wings and fly.

CHAPTER ONE

SETTING UP YOUR BUSINESS

Starting Out on the Right Foot

You are now officially an entrepreneur.

Your brother-in-law may be urging you to incorporate, while your neighbor coaches you on how to avoid taxes. You are puzzled by EINs, ISBNs, and DBAs. Which organizational steps make sense, and what are disproportionate to the size of your business? After all, you don't know whether you will sell a hundred books or a million.

Let's refer to CAM, our main goals.

C	• Control your work
A	• Avoid scams and lawsuits
M	• Maximize tax deductions

In this chapter, I cover

- maintaining control over your work by owning your ISBNs and domain names,
- avoiding legal missteps, particularly with trademarks and sales taxes, and
- separating business finances from personal finances to support income tax deductions for self-publishing expenses.

DO YOU NEED TO INCORPORATE?

Highly unlikely. Businesses incorporate in order to shield the owner's personal assets from business liabilities, but incorporation provides little benefit to an author. The same is true for other entities like limited liability companies (LLCs).

In publishing, your greatest risks are claims of infringement, defamation, and invasion of privacy. These claims are based on your conduct as an *individual,* so forming a corporation or LLC will not help. The corporation is not infringing, *you* are. Besides, forming and maintaining a corporation or other entity costs hundreds of dollars each year. That money is better spent buying business liability and umbrella insurance, which I will discuss later in this chapter.

If you are making net income (revenues less expenses) of $400 of more a year from self-publishing AND the cost of maintaining a corporation or LLC is less than $300 a year in your state, then it might be worth setting up an entity for tax reasons. In that case, check with a tax professional.

Your business will be a *sole proprietorship.* Despite its name, a sole proprietorship may be owned by you alone or by you and your spouse. You do not have to file any documents with governmental entities to create a sole proprietorship. You do not need to give your sole proprietorship a business name, although I recommend that you do so. You create a sole proprietorship simply by going into business.

If you are combining efforts to produce and share income with one or more other people (other than your spouse), then you are forming a "general partnership." Like a sole proprietorship, forming a general partnership requires no governmental filing. The partnership is created as soon as the partners agree to combine efforts to earn a profit. Your agreement may be verbal or in writing, but I recommend you capture it in writing. Writing down your partnership or collaboration agreement forces you and your partners to discuss issues you may be avoiding. For guidance on the questions to ask, see *Chapter Nine: Collaborations.*

HOW TO CHOOSE A COMPANY OR IMPRINT NAME

Even if your self-publishing business is a sole proprietorship, I recommend you give the business a company name, commonly known as a DBA, short for "doing business as." Operating under a DBA name encourages you and others to see the venture as a business.

Your company name will also be your *imprint name*, and you will list it as the "publisher" of your book online, in catalogues, and on the book itself. An imprint name will make it less obvious that your book is self-published. Many bookstores, reviewers, bloggers, contests, and readers refuse to consider self-published work.

Some bloggers criticize self-publishers for using imprint names by claiming they mislead readers into thinking a book is traditionally vetted and published. Hogwash. Think of all the small businesses you know: the local flower shop, the wedding photographer, the physical therapist, the fruit seller at the farmers' market. Many of them use DBAs even if they are a mom-and-pop company. Why not you? Your self-publishing venture is no less legitimate a business.

Choosing a company and imprint name is a creative process. You could use your personal name, such as "Helen Sedwick Publications," which does not say much. Optimally, the name will imply some characteristic or promise about your books, such as romance (Passion Press), adventure (Kick-Ass Books), travel (Rickshaw Riders), or life-changing insights (Next Chapter Publications). My novel, *Coyote Winds*, is set in the American West, so I chose Ten Gallon Press as the name of my imprint. I tried dozens of other names, such as Prairie Winds Press and Coyote Publications, but I researched their availability and found they were already in use.

Your imprint name may include the word "company," but should *not* include corp., corporation, or inc., unless you have set it up as a corporation.

HOW TO CHECK THE AVAILABILITY OF A NAME

Before you fall in love with a company and imprint name, search the market. Avoid any name that infringes on the trademark rights of others. For U.S. registered trademarks, start with the database at the U.S. Patent and Trademark Office (USPTO).

Trademark law is tricky. If you find a registered trademark that is the same or similar to your dream name, do not despair. Most of the time, you may use a name similar to an existing trademark as long as you do not *"create a likelihood of confusion in the mind of the consumer as to the source of the product."* What does that mean? Here's an example:

I searched the trademark "Goody Two Shoes" and found one "live" registration by MaxWax Inc., for a "hair removal service using wax or sugar that removes hair from women or men up to two inches inside the bikini line." If you named your imprint Goody Two Shoes, you are highly unlikely to be infringing on MaxWax's trademark because your products and services are so different. However, if you find your dream name being used as a trademark for books or anything related to publications, communications, or education, keep brainstorming. If you use it as an imprint name, you are asking for legal trouble.

Search your state's trademark database. As of this writing, the California Secretary of State's office will search up to two names by phone and more by mail. In other states, you may be able to search online.

However, do not use a well-known or strong trademark such as McDonald's, Sears, or Exxon, even if you would be using it on a noncompeting product. Owners of strong marks have the right to challenge any similar trademark that may "dilute" the value of their trademark, regardless of the product or service. No matter how tempted you are to do battle with giants, avoid this fight. Those companies have lawyers who will make your life miserable. You are better off using your time and energy for writing your next book.

To find unregistered trademarks, start with Internet searches using Google, Bing, and other search engines. As you settle on a name, check several search engines since one may show results that the others missed. If you find a company using your dream imprint name as a trademark, apply the *likelihood of confusion* test. If the company is selling auto parts, then using the same or a similar name for a book imprint is not likely to cause confusion and be considered trademark infringement.

Search domain names. Try various spellings and misspellings. See where people land if they type your domain name incorrectly. If the domain name for your imprint name is not available, try adding other words such as *press, publications,* or *books.*

Once you have settled on a shortlist of names, search your county's DBA listings. Many counties have online databases. By law in most states, you cannot use a DBA already in use in your county regardless of whether or not your businesses are different. I do not know how often these laws are enforced.

CLAIMING YOUR IMPRINT NAME

Fictitious Business Name Statement. Once you have decided on your company/imprint name, file a Fictitious Business Name Statement (FBN Statement) with the county where your business will be located. Some people will call this a DBA (doing business as) filing. It is a simple and inexpensive task.

An Internet search of "Fictitious Business Name" and the name of your county will pull up services that handle the recording and publication for a small fee. The cost is typically less than $100. Doing it yourself won't save much money, so I recommend you hire a company to handle your FBN filing.

In California, the filing involves (1) recording an FBN Statement with the county recorder and (2) publishing a notice in a local newspaper once a week for four weeks. Most states have similar requirements. You need to renew your FBN Statement every five years.

Why bother filing an FBN Statement? If you get a check made out to your imprint name, you will have trouble cashing it unless you show your bank a recorded FBN Statement. With an FBN Statement, you may also set up bank accounts and obtain credit cards in the imprint name, which simplifies keeping track of your self-publishing expenses and income.

Trademark protection. If you are selling your books under an imprint name, that name is your *trademark*. A trademark identifies goods and services in commerce. In contrast, your ownership in the *contents* of the book is a copyright. I provide a more in-depth discussion about copyrights in *Chapter Four: Getting Rights Right.*

Should you register your imprint name as a trademark with the USPTO? It is not required. You will own a common-law trademark as soon as you offer your books for sale under your imprint name.

Federal registration has several advantages. It puts the world on notice of your claim of ownership of the mark. It creates a legal presumption of ownership nationwide, and it gives you the exclusive right to use the mark on or in connection with the goods or services set forth in the registration. You may file an *intent to use* (ITU) application to trademark your imprint name before you actually offer your books for sale. The USPTO has various publications to help and befuddle you.

Foreign trademark registration is also available. The Community Trade Mark System covers European Union member states, and the Madrid System for the International Registration of Trademarks permits a trademark registrant to use one basic application to register the trademark in various countries.

Trademark protection comes at a cost. Currently, the application fees for U.S. registration are $325 and up. And the USPTO may decide your imprint name does not qualify for trademark registration, and they do not return your fee. You may need a trademark lawyer to assist you, another expense.

Registering your imprint name as a trademark could be overkill.

How Much Legal Protection Do You Need? Let's pause for a moment and discuss proportionality. Are you paying for a ten-foot cement wall when a picket fence will do?

Think of using the law in two ways. One is defensively. You conduct a trademark search as a defensive measure to avoid infringing on the trademark rights of others.

The law is also used offensively (and here I'm using the term to mean to advance strategically, as in football). If you register your trademark, you will have more options for stopping infringement and collecting damages, in other words, going on the offensive.

Consider how much time and money you are willing to spend to stop someone from using a name that infringes on your imprint name. How much are you likely to lose as a result of the infringement compared to the cost of trying to stop it, not only in terms of money, but in time, irritation, and distraction? This question arises with respect to your copyrighted works as well. Most people underestimate the frustrating and consuming nature of litigation.

In other words, you could put off registering your imprint name as a trademark until you see how well your book or books sell.

Domain names. Once you decide on an imprint name, buy the domain name ASAP. It's most helpful to obtain the .com domain, but consider buying .net, .info, and other tags as well. They are small and worthwhile investments. Also, buy domains for your name (or pen name) and your book title (or alternative tentative titles). If those domain names are already taken, try adding descriptive words. For example, if my name were taken, I might try the domain name HelenSedwickwriter.com. Look into alternate spellings, especially if you use one of those British words like *flavour, labour, mum, towards.*

Most hosting providers offer packages that include a small website, email, and forwarding (so you can direct your various domain addresses to one website). For additional fees, many hosting sites will provide credit-card processing, design services, and search engine optimization (SEO). (SEO means *search engine optimization* and increases the likelihood that your site or blog will rank high in Internet searches.)

Private registration. If you register a domain, then your name, address, phone number, and email are searchable on whois.net. Disclosing your name won't matter for your author website, but purchase Private Registration from the hosting provider for your imprint website to reduce the chances people will see that you are both writer and publisher.

SSL CERTIFICATES

If you will be taking credit cards and transacting business on your website, then purchase an SSL Certificate, which will ensure that data is encrypted. If you are processing sales through PayPal or a similar site, you do not need an SSL Certificate; they provide the encryption and security.

FEDERAL EMPLOYEE IDENTIFICATION NUMBER (EIN)

Here is something most people don't know. You may, and in fact should, obtain a separate Federal Employer Identification Number (EIN) for your self-publishing business, even if it is a sole proprietorship, even if you never have employees, and even if you sell only a few books. An EIN is equivalent to a Social Security Number for your business. If you have a separate EIN, then you won't have to give Amazon and other sellers your Social Security Number. They will accept your EIN instead. You may obtain an EIN whether or not you operate under a DBA or imprint name.

Be sure you go directly to the IRS website to apply for your EIN: www.irs.gov. Sham sites that look like the IRS site are popping up every day. They ask for your Social Security Number, mother's maiden name, birthday—all the tools for stealing your identity. Scary stuff.

PURCHASING YOUR OWN ISBNS

If you plan to make your book available at bookstores, libraries, and online retailers, then each version of your book should have its own ISBN. An ISBN, short for International Standard Book Number, is a unique identifier for a particular version of a book in a specific format. In the United States, all ISBNs are issued by R.R. Bowker.

Many self-publishing experts recommend that writers purchase a package of at least ten ISBNs. You will be able to use them with any print-on-demand (POD) company or your self-publishing service company (SPSC) provider. Here is the price list from the Bowker site as of September 2014:

One ISBN	$125
Ten ISBNs	$295
100 ISBNs	$575
1,000 ISBNs	$1000

Your POD or SPSC provider is likely to offer you free or low-price ISBNs. Obtaining ISBNs through your POD or SPSC provider has its drawbacks. As of this writing, if you use one of CreateSpace's free ISBNs, then the publisher of your book will be listed as CreateSpace Independent Publishing Platform, which is like screaming that you are *a self-publishing novice.* If you buy one of CreateSpace's Custom ISBNs for $10, then your imprint will be listed as the publisher. While this sounds like the perfect solution, you may use the Custom ISBN *only* for copies provided by CreateSpace. If you change POD providers, you may not take the ISBN with you.

At the beginning of this chapter, I said one of your goals is to control your work and everything associated with it, including the cover, the website, and the ISBNs. If you purchase an ISBN through your POD or SPSC provider, then, typically, they will control that ISBN. If you change providers, you may have to get a new ISBN.

Since many book rankings are tied to ISBNs, switching the ISBN could tank your rankings.

CreateSpace also offers a transportable, Custom Universal ISBN for $99. That is for a single ISBN. Since you will need several ISBNs, it makes more sense to buy a package of ten directly from Bowker for $295 in your imprint name.

Why ten ISBNs? You will need one for each version of the book, each format, and every translation. You will use one ISBN for your paperback, a different ISBN for the e-book, and another one for the audio book. Here is a list of when you need to use a new ISBN:

Hardcover	Yes
New publisher	Yes
New size	Yes
Translation	Yes
Adding a preface, introduction, appendix, or substantial new content	Yes
New book in a series	Yes
Excerpts and supplemental materials if sold separately	Yes
Fixing typos	No
Price change	No

Substantially redesigned cover	Yes
New edition	Yes
Audiobook	Yes

ISBNs are not transferable, so do not buy an ISBN from a friend or through an advertisement. If you purchase an ISBN in the secondary market, there is a risk that the number could be canceled on you or that your book will be listed as published by someone else.

ISBNs are not recyclable. If a version of your book goes out of print, you may not reuse its ISBN for another version or book.

The Bowker site offers a variety of products and services, with links to other providers and companies. Don't jump into those without researching your options. While Bowker may be the only source for buying ISBNs, the other services it offers are widely available. Shop around before you commit.

RESALE OR SELLER'S CERTIFICATE

Unless you live in a state that does not charge sales tax, you are required to obtain a resale certificate, sometimes called a seller's permit. A resale certificate is different from your EIN, your ISBNs, your business license number, or any other number. Welcome to the number-filled world of small business!

In California, you apply online with the State Board of Equalization. Each state has an equivalent agency. The applications are easy. I recommend that the resale certificate be in the name of your imprint and that you use your new EIN, again, to separate your business activities from your personal ones.

Once you provide a copy of your resale certificate or your certificate number to CreateSpace, Lightning Source, or other POD provider, you won't have to pay sales tax on books *you intend to resell.* When you resell the books to your customers at book fairs and through your website, you may be obligated to pay sales tax to the state in which the transaction takes place, although you may charge it to your buyers. Calculating, collecting, and paying sales tax is a headache. I will discuss more details in *Chapter Eight: Taxes.*

OBTAIN AN LCCN

An LCCN is a Library of Congress Control Number. It is free, and you should obtain one for your book BEFORE you release it. So you don't forget, obtain the LCCN as soon as you have assigned the book an ISBN. Your SPSC, CreateSpace and other POD providers will obtain an LCCN number for you for a fee, typically $50 or so, but you could get one yourself and save the expense. The process is quite easy.

Go to the Library of Congress Preassigned Control Number Program (http://www.loc.gov/publish/pcn/) and click on *Open an Account.* Fill out the form and submit it, and you will be e-mailed an account number and a password. Go back to the site and sign on using this account number and password. You will fill out yet another form specifically for your book. Submit that form, and the LCCN will come to you via email.

The website states that each step of the process may take up to a week, but when registering this Handbook, I received the LCCN emails within 30 minutes. After obtaining the number, you send one copy of your book to the Library of Congress. The mailing address will be in the email confirming your registration and LCCN.

BUSINESS LICENSES

Many cities and counties require businesses to obtain a business license. You'll have to do your own research on this item. The Small Business Administration website will help you search your local jurisdiction. Also, do a web search for "business license" and the city, town, county, and state where your business is located. Often, a city or state website will have a section to help you with this process. Check for such section titles as Doing Business, Starting a Business, or Business Portal.

BANK ACCOUNTS

To keep finances straight, I recommend you open a separate business bank account to cover expenses and to deposit income. You may also find it useful to get a credit card and debit card in your company name. You will need your FBN Statement to open any account in a name other than your own.

Alternatively, you may use your personal bank accounts to deposit income and pay expenses for your self-publishing business. There is no rule against it. However, keep track of your self-publishing income and expenses for tax purposes.

MERCHANT ACCOUNTS

You will find it handy to set up business accounts with USPS, UPS, and FedEx. Having separate accounts will help you keep track of your expenses for tax reasons, and many providers offer lower rates and better service to their business customers. Go to their websites and register. Most will ask for your credit card information and Social Security Number. Provide your EIN (if you have one) instead of your personal Social Security Number.

When you start selling books, sign up for PayPal Here, Square, or a similar service that permits you to accept PayPal, debit, and credit card payments by using a little gizmo that plugs into your cell phone. As of the writing of this book, the fee is 2.75% (give or take) of the charge, but there is no minimum monthly fee. This is a bargain compared to traditional bank credit-card accounts.

RECORDKEEPING

I encounter the following far too often: A client contacts me in a panic. Her publisher has gone out of business, or her freelancer refuses to deliver the final product, or his self-publishing service company charged an extra $1,000 on his credit card, or a letter arrived accusing him of using an image without permission, but he or she can't find a copy of the contract, license, receipt, or correspondence. The typical explanation: *"I never thought anything would go wrong."* Without a contract and the correspondence surrounding it, the task of sorting out the mess is made a thousand times more difficult, and potentially more expensive.

Keep good contract and financial records. While filing is almost everyone's least favorite task, decent records are critical for protecting your rights, getting what you have bargained for, and saving money at tax time. As I will discuss further in *Chapter Eight: Taxes,* when it comes to tax audits, more people are penalized for losing receipts than for cheating. Don't be one of them.

Dedicate a file drawer or box, real or virtual, to your self-publishing business long before your book hits the shelves. Keep the following:

Contracts and licenses: Retain copies of all agreements with your freelancers, publishing companies, webhosts, advertising/social media companies, and POD providers as well as related correspondence, especially if it contains assurances, explanations, and offers.

Keep receipts and licenses for images, fonts, lyrics, and other content. Most online contracts and licenses have a print-friendly version, but if not, print out the webpage showing the relevant terms or save a screenshot. Note the date the webpage or contract was saved.

I cannot emphasize enough the importance of decent record-keeping. If you ever get hit with a lawyer letter demanding $2,000 for the unauthorized use of an image, think how good it will feel to whip out the paid-up license from your file and send it off to that pesky lawyer.

Financial records: Tracking income and expenses can be as simple as maintaining folders (virtual or printed) full of receipts. Or use software such as QuickBooks. Online sites provide basic bookkeeping templates for free or at a low cost. Do a search online for "small-business bookkeeping," and you'll find options and reviews.

Retain records to reflect your *income* and *expenses*, including

- royalties, whether paid by check or electronic transfers into your bank account,
- direct sales and speaking fees,
- office supplies and postage,
- magazine subscriptions,
- telephone charges,
- printing costs for business cards, bookmarks, and post-cards,
- advertising costs,
- costs for design, video editing, manuscript editing, and analytics software,
- fees and royalties paid for fonts, images, music, etc.,
- writing club dues,

- website hosting and online backup costs,
- subscription costs for online services such as HootSuite,
- payments to freelancers, such as your web designer, editor, copyeditor, cover designer, and publicist,
- cost of books sent to reviewers or given away in promotions,
- contest entry fees, and
- copyright registration fees.

Whatever method you use, keep up with it. Once your book is launched, you may deduct many of these expenses, including those paid in the years prior to your book's release. Our tax code encourages people to start new businesses by permitting deductions. Keep records so you can take advantage of these offsets.

INSURANCE

Liability insurance. When you publish a book, post on your blog, or comment on the Internet, you are exposing yourself to a new set of risks, such as copyright and trademark infringement, invasion of privacy, defamation, and other horrors. Can you get insurance to cover claims, attorney fees, and legal damages? Maybe. The availability of coverage varies state by state, policy by policy.

Your homeowner's insurance and umbrella coverage may provide some coverage for defamation claims arising from your negligence, meaning you took reasonable measures to make truthful statements, but ended up being wrong. Your homeowner's insurance, however, might not cover business pursuits, in which case you may have to purchase a separate business insurance package. Ask your insurance agent.

Of course, these policies are unlikely to help if you *knowingly* make a false and defamatory statement. You'll be on your own.

Large publishers purchase broader coverage called *media liability insurance*. Writers' organizations, such as The Author's Guild, have arranged for discounted policies for their members. The premiums are so high ($1500 to $5000 per year) that media liability insurance doesn't make sense for most self-publishers. This may change in the future. As more people self-publish, I hope carriers will offer media liability coverage at more affordable rates.

Property insurance. If you will be stocking inventory at your home, check with your renters or homeowners insurance agent about how much inventory is covered by your existing policy. If you are storing thousands of copies at your home—or a storage facility—it may be worth paying for optional coverage (known as an *endorsement*) to cover losses from fire, theft, and other typical risks.

CROWDFUNDING

Producing a well-edited, professionally designed book takes money. If you don't have spare change lying around, how do you finance the upfront costs?

Many writers are using crowdfunding to raise money for editors, designers, and production and promotional expenses. In crowdfunding, the writer seeks contributions online. Several websites provide platforms for pitching projects and collecting donations. Kickstarter and Indiegogo are probably the most well-known, but others claim to specialize in helping authors as well.

Some crowdfunding sites offer additional services, such a market testing, advertising, and printing. (Watch out for the fees on the extra services.) Some charge a percentage of the amount raised, while others charge a flat monthly fee. Some crowdfunding venues are based on the *all-or-nothing* model, meaning the author collects nothing unless a certain dollar target is achieved. Others do not have a minimum threshold, and the author keeps whatever is raised. Still others offer you the choice. Read the fine print.

As a writer, I find crowdfunding an exciting resource. As a lawyer, I find it full of dangerous pitfalls. Here are some thoughts on avoiding these pitfalls.

When you solicit money from other people, *do not call it an investment.* If you are selling an investment, then you are selling a security (like a stock or bond), subject to a complex array of federal and state laws. Yes, even if you are raising $2,500, you are selling securities that require registration and detailed disclosure statements. There are exemptions from the registration requirements, particularly if you are raising money exclusively from family and friends and only in small amounts. But if you will be soliciting funds from anyone and everyone on an online site, call the funds *contributions*, not investments or loans.

You may have heard that the JOBS (Jumpstart Our Business Startups) Act legalized crowdfunding. In theory, the law will expand the opportunities for people to invest in crowdfunding ventures. However, the rules are so complex and technical, the exemption is unusable.

Do not say the donations are tax deductible. Many people hear the word "donation" and assume it is tax deductible. Not the case. Unless you are a nonprofit entity that has applied for and received tax-exempt status from the IRS, the donations are not deductible by the donor. Better yet, avoid the word *donation* altogether and call the transfers *contributions.*

Contributions may be taxable income. From what I have read, the IRS has not decided whether funds raised through crowdfunding are taxable income or nontaxable gifts. The more cautious approach treats contributions as taxable income because they are funds obtained in pursuit of a business venture.

If you have deductions for expenses at least equal to the contributions received, you may offset this income.

Sales tax may also apply. If you are offering to send donors copies of your book in exchange for contributions, then you are "selling" the book and owe sales tax on that sale.

Bottom line: Nothing is simple.

SETTING UP YOUR BUSINESS CHECKLIST

Let's review. At this point, you have founded your own company and taken the steps to

- ✓ choose and protect your company/imprint name (DBA),
- ✓ engage a service to record and publish your Fictitious Business Name Statement,
- ✓ obtain domain names,
- ✓ register for an EIN,
- ✓ purchase a package of ten ISBNs,
- ✓ register for a Seller's Certificate,
- ✓ apply for a business license, if needed,
- ✓ open bank accounts and credit cards in your company name,
- ✓ set up merchant accounts,
- ✓ line up insurance, and
- ✓ explore crowdfunding.

You are ready to go into business. Now let's look at the options for transforming your manuscript into a book.

CHAPTER TWO

MOVING FROM MANUSCRIPT TO BOOK

A Dream Comes True

Unless you are amazingly talented or have a collection of fabulous and gifted friends, you will need a team of professionals to transform your manuscript into a book. Before you gasp at the expense, look in the mirror and ask yourself how much you are willing to invest to transform your dream into a reality. Spend what you can, as wisely as you can. The odds of making a profit are slim, but the nonmonetary rewards are substantial. As they say about drinking, spend responsibly.

HOW MUCH WILL SELF-PUBLISHING COST?

Anywhere between $200 and $30,000 depending on

- whether you are publishing an e-book, a paperback, and/or a hardcover,
- how much you do yourself, and
- how much advertising and marketing you buy.

Top Priority: Spend what is necessary to make your manuscript as good as it can be, which means strong editing. The number-one problem with self-published books is that they are released too soon.

Many have potential, but sketchy character development, rambling plots, and sputtering endings hold them back, all problems that could have been solved had the writer endured a few more rewrites with the help of a professional editor.

Don't publish your book before it's ready. That is the most expensive mistake of all.

SELF-PUBLISHING SERVICE COMPANIES VS. DOING IT YOURSELF

You have two main pathways for converting your manuscript into a print book and/or e-book:

- Engage a self-publishing service company (SPSC) to do everything from editing to distributing your book.
- Do it yourself (DIY) by hiring editors, designers, and other professionals, and then uploading your print-ready files to a POD provider such as CreateSpace and/or Lightning Source (or its new affiliate, IngramSpark).

You may also mix the two approaches, since most SPSCs have a la carte menus and many POD providers offer editorial, design, and marketing services as add-ons. You could hire a self-publishing consultant or coach to walk you through the process. Literary agents are also jumping in and offering to manage the self-publishing process for writers—for a percentage, of course.

In the past, people referred to self-publishing companies as *vanity presses*, but vanity presses work on a different business model. Typically they require authors to buy large quantities of their own books, often at inflated prices.

Since the term *vanity press* has become pejorative, these companies now call themselves *hybrid, subsidy, co-op* or *equity* presses. Some require you to submit your manuscript for consideration, as if they were traditional presses. They flatter you by accepting your work. Don't buy it. While they may be weeding out the obscene or defaming work, the flattery is intended to loosen your wallet.

I recommend avoiding the vanity press model. Your money will go farther by using a SPSC or POD to produce your book.

Offset vs. POD Printing. For this chapter, I am assuming that you or your SPSC will be using a print-on-demand (POD) process to produce your books instead of traditional, offset printing. Offset printing is preferable for a work requiring precise, high-quality printing, paper, and ink, such as a photography or art book, but it is too expensive for print runs of less than 500 copies. Few self-publishers use offset printing.

POD books are produced one copy at a time using high-end laser printers, which is cheaper for small print runs. You will have various options about trim sizes, but few choices about paper or binding. POD books are not as high quality as books produced with offset printing, but they are higher quality than the mass-market paperbacks you find at grocery stores.

The POD process is flexible, which is important for an independent author. You might tweak (or entirely redo) your cover, title, and interior contents if sales (or reviews) indicate that revisions are warranted. POD printing is an affordable way to try new looks and approaches a few copies at a time. After all, who needs 1,000 outdated books languishing in the garage next to the abandoned stair climber?

SELF-PUBLISHING SERVICE COMPANIES (SPSCS)

Dozens of SPSCs offer hundreds of self-publishing packages that include editing, design, distribution, and marketing services. The packages start at a few hundred dollars and run as high as $35,000. The bigger companies include Abbott Press, Blurb, BookLocker, Dog Ear Publishing, Lulu, Mill City Press, Outskirts Press, and Xulon Press. Author Solutions (now owned by Penguin Random House) also runs AuthorHouse, Balboa Press, CrossBooks, iUniverse, Palibrio, Trafford, WestBow Press, and Xlibris among others. Some SPSCs have good reputations; others do not. For instance, AuthorHouse has been hit with lawsuits alleging breach of contract. I will provide suggestions on how to research the reputation of an SPSC below.

Self-publishing packages vary widely and include some or all of the following:

- editing,
- cover design,
- interior formatting, including graphics and photos,
- ISBN, LCCN, and bar codes,
- copyright registration,
- e-book conversion,
- listing and distribution through Amazon, Barnes & Noble, Ingram, Baker & Taylor, and international sellers,
- acceptance of book returns from retailers,
- website and blog design and hosting,
- search engine optimization (SEO),
- promotional materials such as bookmarks, business cards, and posters,
- press releases, promotional copy, and author bios,
- blog tours,
- book trailer videos, and
- marketing consultations and services.

To add to the dizzying array of choices, if you speak to a salesperson at any of these companies, you will hear of special options, limited-time offers, and personalized service.

How do you choose which company, which package, which price? Will a $600 custom cover sell more books than a $150 cover? Will editing at two cents per word be more thorough than editing at one cent per word? Will your editor have real-world publishing experience or be an English major struggling through her first job? How do you measure quality and reliability? The choices are overwhelming.

Don't despair. There is a much simpler approach, at least for narrowing your choices.

Let's refer back to CAM, especially the C, Control. The key question is *which SPSC provides you with the most control over your work, particularly the pricing of your print book.*

Pricing? Isn't that putting the cart in front of the horse? What about editing and design? Print quality? They matter, but only if your book is competitively priced.

The harsh reality is that most of your sales will be through three channels:

- e-book (predominantly Kindle)
- online through Amazon, Barnes & Noble.com, etc.
- sales you make yourself at author events and through your website

Your book is unlikely to be carried by brick-and-mortar stores no matter how well executed. The stores won't sacrifice shelf space to an unknown author. And the distribution and discounting system works against self-publishing authors, as I will explain in *Chapter Five: Marketing and Distribution.* Even famous self-publishing hits like *Fifty Shades of Grey* broke out first as e-books.

Bottom line: Pick the SPSC that allows you to list your print book at the lowest retail price and permits you to purchase copies at the lowest author price.

Retail pricing: Some SPSCs set the retail price for your print book unrealistically high. One company claims its high pricing is author friendly because it increases your potential royalties. Forget it. You may have a fabulous book, perfectly edited, with a stunning cover and interior, but if it is priced at $20 alongside bestsellers priced at $15, $12, or $8, no one will buy it. To market your book successfully, the price must be competitive. I would stay away from any SPSC that will price your book out of the market.

Author pricing: Choose an SPSC that will sell your books to you at a reasonable author price. As an indie author, you will be selling books directly at readings, school visits, conferences, and through your website. You will also give away dozens, maybe hundreds, of copies to reviewers, bloggers, friends, and family. Overpaying for these books will swallow your profit.

The author price should be the actual printing costs plus a reasonable markup (15-20%) and not a discount from the retail price. Why pay more for copies of your own book because the SPSC sets the retail price at $18 instead of $10? The printing costs are the same. You have already paid the SPSC hundreds, if not thousands, of dollars for design, editorial, and marketing services. You deserve better.

In my opinion, an SPSC that sets a high retail price for your book is not expecting to make money by selling it to the public. They are going to make money selling to *you*, the author. If they set the retail price of your book at $19.95, then offer to sell you copies at a 30-percent discount, you will pay $13.96 per copy, plus another $2 to $3 for shipping and handling. That's probably two to three times the SPSC's actual printing costs.

For a detailed comparison of various SPSCs, look into *The Fine Print of Self-Publishing* by Mark Levine, now in its fifth edition. Levine compares the packages, costs, pricing, markups, and contracts of SPSCs and POD providers in detail. (Note: Levine operates his own SPSC, and some people claim his book is merely an advertisement, but I found the book informative and valuable.)

I tried to duplicate Levine's work by comparing the retail and author prices for a hypothetical 250-page, 6" x 9", black-and-white trade paperback on standard paper. It was not easy.

According to Levine, the cost for POD printing of my hypothetical book is $0.015 per page plus $0.90 for a color cover, so $4.65 per copy. I went to the websites of various SPSCs to determine whether they would set the retail price and if they charged high printing markup on author copies. The information was often difficult to locate, but eventually I found a few examples. As of December 2013, for my hypothetical book

- AuthorHouse fixed the retail price at $19.99, and the author price was $13.96 per copy for orders of 24 or fewer copies.
- Dog Ear Press would not fix the retail price, and its author price was $6.28 per copy.
- Mill City Press (owned by Levine) would not fix the retail price, and its author price was $4.65 per copy.
- CreateSpace would not fix the retail price, and its author price is $3.85 per copy.

This is a significant spread and worth calculating before choosing any SPSC. Levine's *The Fine Print of Self-Publishing* covers many more companies and options.

OTHER CRITERIA FOR CHOOSING AN SPSC

SPSCs frequently change their packages, pricing, contracts, and web-sites. What I describe today may not apply tomorrow. But no matter when you are comparing SPSCs, look for the following:

Author-friendly website. Be wary of any company if its website does not provide an easy way to calculate the price of publishing packages, optional add-ons, royalties, retail pricing, and the author price assuming different options such as page count. If the website states that pricing, royalties, and such cannot be determined until your manuscript is reviewed or formatted (and typically after you have given them your credit card number and paid a nonrefundable amount), move on to another website and another company that provides you more transparency and control.

Easy termination. You should have the right to terminate the relationship following not more than 30 days' notice delivered via email. None of this *certified mail, return receipt* nonsense. After termination, the provider may have the right to sell off its existing inventory, but that's it. It should not have the right to continue to print and sell your book, even if such rights are nonexclusive. If a traditional publisher were interested in your work, they would want to (or want you to) buy out your former SPSC before they penned any deal with you.

Delivery of production files. If you terminate your relationship with an SPSC, then it should deliver to you the final production files of your cover and interior at no or low cost. **Not PDFs of your print-ready files, not digital files, but the actual, functional production files in Adobe InDesign or comparable format.** It is outrageous for an SPSC to hold onto these files after you've paid for the design, editing, and layout work. You own the work product. They cannot reuse it. As I have said before, *control* your work. If you move your book to a new printer without the production-ready files, then new files will have to be created *at considerable cost to you.*

Easy-to-calculate royalties. As I mentioned earlier, I would be suspicious of any company that did not have a royalty calculator on its website. How can you compare one company against another if you cannot compare potential royalties?

Size. While big is not necessarily better, small may be worse. Small SPSC and publishing companies raise solvency risks. Many run out of money and shut down, despite the best of artistic and business intentions. When they fail, you may not get the services you paid for; you may lose your production files, your royalties, and, in the worst-case scenario, your publishing rights, since those may now belong to the SPSC's creditors, a nightmare situation that calls for you to consult an attorney. Be cautious about engaging a small, unfunded SPSC or publishing company. If you decide to work with one, revise the contract to provide that should they cease operations, the contract and all licenses of your work terminate immediately and automatically.

Reputation. Research the reputation of any provider before you sign up, starting with websites like Predators & Editors, Absolute Write Water Cooler, and Writers Beware. Reviews are available at *The Independent Publishing Magazine* site. Also, check with the Better Business Bureau. I have read authors' complaints about SPSCs inserting typos into books, and then charging the author to make corrections, not once, but repeatedly. Every company will have its share of unhappy customers, so sort through the complaints to try to get a sense of which ones are legitimate. If you find multiple reports from unhappy customers, stay away.

I do not want to scare you away from using an SPSC. Some companies offer reasonable deals and enjoy solid reputations. They permit you to control the process and the result. Do your homework before you commit.

DO-IT-YOURSELF WITH A POD PROVIDER

Instead of hiring an SPSC, you could engage your own team and act as your own publisher, similar to being your own general contractor for a home remodel. If you are on a tight budget, you could do much of the design and layout work on your own or through trades with other book experts.

POD and e-book distributors, such as CreateSpace, Lightning Source, and Lulu for print books, and SmashWords and Kindle Direct Publishing (KDP) for e-books, are geared toward the DIY self-publisher. IngramSpark was launched in 2013 and will probably become a heavyweight in both e-book and printed-book production and distribution.

To use a POD and e-book distributor, you and your team create print-ready or e-book-ready cover and interior files, meeting the technical specifications of each site, for example, size, DPI (dots-per-inch, a measure of clarity and resolution), and file format. You upload the files, and the POD and e-book distributor take care of the rest. Their websites provide information about formatting, conversion, and distribution; and offer downloadable templates for various trim sizes and binding options. If your e-book file meets SmashWords' requirements, they will convert the file into the various e-book formats and deliver it to Apple's iBookstore, Barnes & Noble for Nook, Diesel, Scribd, Oyster, and other channels for digital sales and distribution.

CreateSpace and some other POD providers also offer editing, design, and marketing, available a la carte and in packages, making them SPSCs as well.

Potentially, your earnings will be higher if you go the DIY route since you are not paying the SPSC its profit. You'll have control over design, timing, pricing, discount rates, costs, and the production files.

But DIY involves hundreds of decisions. Whom do you hire and for how much? What's the best trim size? What colors will make your cover pop? What font conveys the correct tone for your book? How do you price your e-book? What do you say on the back cover? If you break out in a sweat when making decisions, DIY may not be for you. You may be better off working with a reputable SPSC.

Personally, I chose DIY for *Coyote Winds* and the *Self-Publisher's Legal Handbook*. I'll confess, I am something of a control freak. An occupational hazard.

In the next chapter, I'll walk you through finding, hiring, and working with your publishing team. Most of these professionals are a pleasure to work with because they love what they do.

WHAT TO LOOK FOR IN YOUR CONTRACTS

Whether you engage an SPSC or go the DIY route, you will be entering into a contract. Before you click on I AGREE or I ACCEPT on the Services Agreement—STOP. This is a contract you must read.

Don't assume all companies are author friendly, honest, and fair. Some set high markups that swallow profit. Others claim exclusive rights to your work for the life of the copyright. Print out the contract, grab a pen, and then search for and circle the following terms.

Contract Term	SPSC/POD Terms That Are Acceptable	SPSC/POD Terms to Avoid
License	• Nonexclusive rights • Limited to print and digital rights • Worldwide rights, but excluding any area the author designates • Right to display, sell, fulfill, deliver, and promote the book • Right to use your name, image, and bio in connection with the book	• Exclusive rights • Any option or claim to subsidiary, audio, movie, stage, merchandising, or other rights • Any option or right of first refusal on derivative works, past or future works, and future formats or income

Ownership	• You retain ownership of all content you create. • You own the finished cover and interior designs. • The SPSC or POD retains ownership of its own templates, proprietary promotional materials, and software.	• Any claim of ownership to your content or the finished book
Refunds	• Design and editorial fees are refundable in whole or in part if you are not satisfied. • If you terminate, unused fees are refundable.	• Entire fee is paid in advance and is non-refundable.
Author's royalty rate	• Based on retail price • Easily calculated	• Based on net price, especially if "net" is not well-defined • No online royalty calculator
Retail pricing	• You choose suggested retail price Some companies reserve the right to discount your retail price, but pay royalties based upon your approved retail price.	• They set retail price or require a high minimum price.
Recurring fees	• Small fees for file storage, hosting websites and blog, and other ongoing services	• Hidden fees • Fees for vaguely described additional services
Price of making changes	• Three to five revisions of cover, interior, and other work included in package price • Clearly stated charges for additional revisions	• Few or no revisions included in package • High revision fees • Hidden, unspecified, recurring or excessive charges
Discount rate given to retailers	• You choose discount rate, or it's a fixed number you know upfront.	• They choose discount rate and may change it without notice.

Price of author copies	• Price is reasonable markup (15-20%) above actual printing costs.	• High or undisclosed markup • Price based on discount from retail price, particularly if they choose the retail price

Termination	• Either party may terminate at any time with reasonable notice (no more than 30 days).
	• After termination, they may only:
	  (i) sell off existing inventory,
	  (ii) retain a digital copy to "refresh" digital orders and for archival purposes, and
	  (iii) continue to display your book on their website even if they are not fulfilling orders.
	• On termination, you receive production-ready files of your cover and interior at little or no cost.
		• Any contract that does not clearly state how and when you may terminate
		• Termination fees
		• Any contract that lasts for the life of the copyright
		• Automatic renewals
		• Any right to continue to sell your book after termination
		• They do not provide you with production-ready files of your cover and interior upon termination.

Timing of services	• Clearly stated timeline for services • Timing of turnaround on revisions • Timing of listing of final book on Amazon, etc.	Vague timelines
Author warranties and representations	• You are the sole author. • The work is original. • You have the right to sell all of the content. • You are not infringing on anyone's rights. • The content is not defamatory, libelous, obscene, or unlawful, and does not violate the privacy, right of publicity, or any other rights of others.	• Any warranty about sales volume

ADDITIONAL RED FLAGS

When checking out an SPSC or POD provider, steer clear of

- any company that won't let you see their contract or prices until you provide them personal information and/or your credit card number.

- any company that forces you to talk to a live person to get basic information. If you prefer to talk to a live person, that's great, but you should not be forced to endure a sales talk just to get the basics. These guys are pros at separating you from your money. Call to ask questions, but if they launch into a sales pitch, warn them you will hang up if they don't stop immediately.

- any company that requires you to agree to confidentiality provisions or a so-called "no gossip" policy. If you have a legitimate complaint about these companies, a confidentiality agreement would bar you from warning other writers and posting your experience online, no matter how legitimate.

- any company that engages in bait-and-switch tactics. If you call about a self-publishing package advertised at $399, but by the time you include basic add-ons the price jumps to $1,399, hang up.

In the Addendum, I will annotate and compare the CreateSpace and KDP agreements with an example of an egregious contract from a company I won't name. But believe me, it's a real contract out there ready to snag unsuspecting writers.

MOVING FROM MANUSCRIPT TO BOOK CHECKLIST

At this point, you have decided between the SPSC and DIY process or crafted a combination of the two approaches. You have

- ✓ set a comfortable, but realistic publishing budget,
- ✓ chosen an SPSC that permits you to control retail pricing and discount rates, charges a reasonable price for author copies, returns production-ready files, and has fair contract terms, or
- ✓ elected the DIY route and are ready to engage and manage your own publishing team, and
- ✓ researched the reputation of your SPSC or POD company.

The journey of transforming your project from manuscript to print book and/or e-book now seems less like an impassable mountain road and more like a well-worn path. You are retaining control of your work and your dream. You are metamorphosing from writer to author.

CHAPTER THREE

ENGAGING DESIGNERS, EDITORS, AND OTHER FREELANCERS

The Fun Begins

Your entrepreneurial blood is pumping. Not only are you an author, you are soon to be a publisher, art director, marketer, CEO, CFO, and part-time techie.

Or are you are wondering, *What am I getting myself into? I'm a writer—isn't that enough?*

How are you going to wear so many hats if you have only one head? Hiring, managing, negotiating, correcting, and firing freelancers and other strangers is not your thing. Those SPSC packages are looking better already.

Slow down. Let's take this one step at a time, or as Anne Lamott says, "bird by bird."

HOW TO FIND THE RIGHT PEOPLE

Your goal is to find freelance talent with real-world publishing experience within your genre. Don't hire a self-help editor to revise an historical novel or a racy romance artist to design the cover for a book about grief. Even if the freelancer is willing to expand into new arenas, not on your nickel, please.

Start by asking for recommendations from authors, including traditionally published ones. Find books in your genre and email the writers. Many will respond with information and advice. Check with local writers' groups and organizations, particularly any organization of independent publishers. Post questions on writers' forums and communities. If you get in touch with one freelancer who isn't a good fit, ask for a referral. There's a network of good people out there.

Online sites such as Elance, Freelancer, and VoiceRealm match up freelancers and projects, often by a bidding system. You'll get offers from freelancers worldwide. They will range from rank beginners to seasoned professionals. These sites act as go-betweens for handling payments and approvals.

You will also find designers, editors, and other potential members of your creative team by searching online for "book cover designer" or "book publicist," etc., but read the websites carefully. Be wary of any site that boasts the company "knows the market" or "knocks down doors" or "turns your rough draft into a diamond," but says nothing about the freelancer's work experience. Look for credentials. With the downsizing in the publishing industry, plenty of top-notch editors and designers are available for freelance projects. Don't hire a rookie with a slick website.

Prices will vary widely. Remember the most expensive editor, designer, or publicist may not be the best person for you or your book. But the cheapest may be a greater waste of money. Look for relevant professional experience, good word-of-mouth references, and an aesthetic style that fits your own.

MEET YOUR DIY TEAM

Editor. There are different levels of editorial review ranging from developmental editing (about structure and plot) to copyediting (detailed, line-by-line editing), which is more expensive. The Bay Area Editors' Forum website has a handy explanation of the different editing options and has a search function for finding editors. (http://www.editorsforum.org/what_do_sub_pages/definitions.php)

Before you hire an editor, ask for an edit of a few sample pages. Some editors have no "ear," or their ear is tuned differently than yours. Or they may say your work is so wonderful they have little to add. While that may be flattering, it's not helpful.

The fee for an editor may vary from $500 to $5,000 and up, depending on the length of your manuscript, the editor's experience, and the editorial option you choose.

Copy editor. A copy editor checks grammar, punctuation, and consistency. Do not rely on friends. They won't be nit-picky enough; it's an acquired skill. Communicate with your copy editor about whether you want a light, medium, or heavy copyedit. And make sure to ask if your copy editor's fee includes proofreading. Some copy editors do not proofread unless asked. The fee for a copy editor ranges from $0.015 to $0.050 per word. Some charge by the hour, typically $20 per hour and up.

Indexing, fact-checking, permissions, and/or technical editing. Depending on your project, you may need specialized editorial assistance. Again, the Bay Area Editors' Forum explains these different roles and duties. Fees range from $200 and up for any one of these editorial services.

Cover designer. A good cover tells a story in itself. It catches the reader's eye and communicates the theme of your book, not just in full size, but as a thumbnail image online. Most designers have sample covers on their websites. Many offer ready-made templates at a reasonable price. If you are working on a tight budget or accelerated time frame, ready-made cover templates are an attractive option. Fees range from $10 (for a template) to $5,000, depending on the designer and the complexity of the work.

Interior designer for print books. The designer selects fonts, chapter headings, and other design elements, and lays out each page. A novel is simpler to lay out than a nonfiction book with sidebars, graphs, and charts. Interior design templates are available online. Like ready-made covers, their quality keeps improving. Using a template, you could lay out your own interior yourself, but be prepared to commit hours to it. It is detailed work.

If your project is a nonfiction book with tables, charts, and graphics, consider hiring an *information designer* or *information architect*. They specialize in the layout of information in *infographics*, so it is easier to understand and absorb. Sometimes the work is referred to as *data visualization*. Fees range from $300 to $2,500.

Website and blog designer. You can do this yourself if you have the patience and expertise. There are hundreds of WordPress themes that claim to be user friendly for the non-techie, and there are dozens of books and seminars to walk you through the process. If you hire a designer, ask about ownership and control of the work product. Some website designers retain ownership of the site banner and other design elements, so only they can update your site. Fees range from $50 to $5,000.

Conversion/formatting consultant for e-book formats. If you are publishing a novel without unusual formatting, then you can convert your manuscript into an e-book fairly easily. Delete drop caps and other special codes, and upload the manuscript to Kindle Direct Publishing (KDP). If you have some production experience, you may be able to format your manuscript to the requirements for the SmashWords Premium catalog, iBook, Nook, and other formats.

Otherwise, I recommend you hire a book format or conversion specialist, particularly if your book contains charts, graphs, and photographs, or has special formatting requirements. Typically, the charges are between $50 and $200, depending on the complexity of the project. This is a small price to pay to avoid hours of frustration.

No matter which route you follow, check your book in each format (Kindle, Nook, iPad, Kobo, etc.) as text that looks fine in one version may be chopped up in another.

Book-trailer videographer. Book trailers have become a popular way to generate interest in your project. Many SPSCs and other providers, including CreateSpace, produce trailers. You can make one yourself using Windows Movie Maker or other programs. However, if your video does not appear professional, it may do you more harm than good.

If you make a trailer, be sure you obtain the appropriate rights to all images and music. If you hire someone to create it, your agreement should ensure that you own the video once you pay for it. The cost to hire a videographer may range from $400 to $2,000 and up, depending on the complexity of the trailer.

Publicist. The most important thing you pay for when you hire a publicist is his level of media contacts. If your publicist doesn't have familiarity with—and access to—a range of editors and producers, then your money will not be well spent. Look for a publicist with a track record in your genre, the more focused the better. A generalist is likely to put in thousands of dollars of effort with no valuable result. Fees for a freelance publicist can start at $1,000 per month and go much higher, depending on how long you engage the publicist.

Audiobook producer. This is another big investment and one that's not worth doing unless you produce a professional quality product. If you decide to produce the audiobook book yourself, there are online sites where you can audition and hire voice-over talent.

The cost of creating an audiobook can be anywhere from $0 (if you narrate your book or enter into a royalty-sharing agreement with your narrator) to $2,500, depending on the length of your manuscript.

Social-media consultant. There are experts out there who will help you set up your social media presence, including coaching you on time management and analytic services such as HootSuite, Twylah, Socialoomph, and Social Report. They will write posts and tweets for you, and assist you in choosing keywords and content to improve SEO. (SEO means *search engine optimization* and increases the likelihood that your site or blog will rank high in Internet searches.) They advise you on how to improve *engagement,* the current buzzword in social media. If you are not fluent in the language of social media, these consultants could get your social media brand up and running quickly and efficiently. Fees for a social-media consultant are usually on a per-hour basis, ranging from $50 to $150 per hour.

Photographer. Do not have your spouse take a photo of you in the backyard with the dog. Do not hold your phone at arm's length for a selfie. A headshot session is fun. Get dressed up. Be a character. Be glamorous. Be both. You have worked hard on this book, and now is your moment to shine. Have a blast and get some nice photos of yourself. That's the best non-legal advice I can give. Fees for professional photographers range from $200 to $400.

Massage therapist, cool chardonnay, fuzzy dog, or other stress reducers. Value of these necessities—priceless.

OTHER COSTS

In addition to the expenses of hiring your team, expect to spend money on the following:

Website and email hosting. Websites have become a must-have. Some writers sell a lot of books through their sites. Maintaining your website may cost you between $50 and $100 per year, depending on the size of your website, the number and size of the mailboxes, and other bells and whistles.

ISBN. As I discussed in Chapter One, I recommend you purchase a package of ten ISBNs in the name of your imprint. If this is beyond your budget, get a free or inexpensive ISBN from your POD provider. Remember, however, your book may be listed as published by the POD provider, and if you change your POD provider, you may have to change your book's ISBN. The cost for ten ISBNs from Bowker is $295.

Bookmarks, postcards, business cards, and promotional materials. Bookmarks and business cards are handy to give away at readings and events. Online sites provide templates for building your own materials. Your cover designer and/or website designer might assist you in designing your promotional materials at a reasonable price.

Although it is tempting to order a thousand bookmarks because the price per item drops, order your materials in smaller batches. You may get reviews and blurbs to add to your bookmarks. You may even change your cover or title. Avoid tossing a thousand outdated bookmarks and postcards into the recycling bin. Costs for these items range from $40 to $200.

Shipping (supplies and postage). To save on postage, send out books using media mail. Cost varies with volume.

Paid reviews. This is a controversial subject. Is a review legitimate if you pay for it? The truth is, as a self-published author, you may have to pay reviewers to look at your work. I will discuss paid, unpaid, traded, and bogus reviews in *Chapter Six: Marketing and Distribution*. Costs range from $19 to $575.

Images, music, and other third-party content. Just because an image, article, or piece of music is online does not mean you can use it for free. Why risk infringing on the rights of a fellow artist? There are millions—*yes, millions*—of photographic and illustrated images available for free under Creative Commons licenses or for sale on sites such as Dreamstime.com, iStockPhoto.com, Getty Images, Shutterstock, and Illustrationsource.com. Search stock photos of your subject matter, and you'll find numerous possibilities. The same is true if you're looking for music. And the cost is manageable, typically $5 to $100 per image or sound clip. Read more about buying stock images and music in *Chapter Four: Getting Rights Right.*

Software. Buy some formatting, design, and video-editing programs so you can design your own flyers, bookmarks, book covers, and book videos. I purchased Adobe Elements and have found it extremely worthwhile. The cost for these software programs starts at $50. Some may be "rented" online more economically.

Advertising and promotion. Print ads, online click-throughs, direct-mail postcards, blog tours—the advertising and promotional options are limitless, and so is the potential cost. Target your efforts to reach your most likely readers. Costs depend on the media used. A print ad in *Publisher's Weekly* will cost thousands, while an ad on a blog may cost a fraction of a cent per *click-through.* See more in *Chapter Six: Marketing and Distribution.*

Contests. Contests range from literary awards to outright scams. The submission fees run into the hundreds of dollars, and with some contests all you win are stickers to put on your book. I review criteria for distinguishing between legitimate contests and scams in *Chapter Six: Marketing and Distribution.* Entry fees are anywhere from $0 to $200 for each contest, so choose wisely.

Trade shows and book fairs. As in advertising, choose events that target your most likely readers. Some shows and fairs are free, but most have registration fees ranging from $50 to $1,500.

Free copies. In promoting your book, you will give away copies to bloggers, reviewers, media contacts, friends, relatives, and other writers. To cut down on sending freebies to media, send out query letters and follow up with free books only to those who request a review copy. The cost of sending giveaway books adds up quickly, and there is no use sending a copy to someone who isn't interested. I had the unhappy experience of having review copies of *Coyote Winds* show up as used books on Amazon *before* the book was officially released.

CONTRACT BASICS

You have chosen an editor, book-cover designer, interior designer, photographer, illustrator, audiobook narrator, or other freelance contractor. Now what? How do you spell out your mutual expectations or, to put it in legal language, the *terms of engagement?*

Most likely, your freelancer has a form agreement, which may be only a description on a website or an email. These are acceptable forms of contracts, and they will form binding agreements even if they are 100 percent electronic. However, make sure the agreement covers the following items:

Describe what services are expected: Spell out what you expect the contractor to provide. For example,

- line-by-line editorial review for a _____ book. Describe the project's genre, such as thriller, romance, historical novel, memoir, how-to, or travel book,
- complete copyediting for grammar, typos, continuity, including proofreading,
- internal layout for a specific trim size and/or for an e-book in a list of formats,
- a specified number of rough cover designs, number of revisions, final design in print-ready PDF format and/or Adobe InDesign files, in specified sizes,

- website of x number of pages, images, tabs, links; banners for Facebook, Twitter, etc.,
- timing of deliveries,
- number of revisions included in price; cost of additional revisions, and
- format of final product.

Payments: How much and when? Check, credit card, or PayPal? Is the payment refundable in whole or in part if you are not satisfied? Are there any ongoing payments such as royalties or renewal fees? Any expense reimbursements?

Attribution: Are you required to give your freelancer attribution, for example, "Cover designed by XYZ," "Audiobook narrated by GHJ," or "Photographs by ABC"?

Credits: May the freelancer list you as a client on his website? May he post your cover, illustration, or photo on his website? Clarify whether he must hold off posting your cover until your book is launched. I had the unfortunate surprise of discovering that a designer had posted all his cover design proposals for my project on Twitter and Facebook months ahead of the book's release. So much for confidentiality.

Termination: Either party should have the right to terminate the agreement at any time. If the engagement is not working out, either one of you should be entitled to bail out. It's better to lose some time and money than to stick with a relationship that is not working. Many freelancers include a "kill fee" in their agreement: if you terminate after signing the contract but before the work begins, you agree to pay a fixed amount, typically 5 to 10 percent of the total contract price. This compensates the freelancer for booking you into his schedule. A reasonable kill fee is fair.

Communication: What is the preferred method of communication? Is the freelancer available for telephone calls? Is there a limit on the number of calls?

Rights: The following issues are often ignored, but it is NOT TO YOUR ADVANTAGE to ignore them.

- The freelancer represents and warrants that he has the authority to transfer the final product to you free and clear of any claims of any third party.
- If the freelancer has used anyone else's intellectual property, such as stock music or images, the freelancer has obtained all permissions and licenses necessary to permit you to use them.
- The freelancer's final product (such as illustrations and designs) is exclusively yours. However, if your design incorporates stock images from a site such as Shutterstock or a free image available to anyone through a Creative Commons license, then you will not have exclusive rights to those stock images.

Ownership: Control is once again the guiding principle. You should own or have the exclusive license to the final product, whether it is a website banner, book cover, or author photo. To gain control, the contract must grant to you an ***assignment*** or an ***exclusive license*** to the final product, although it is typical to permit freelancers to display it as part of their portfolios.

Do not rely on the phrase *work-for-hire*. It is a shorthand expression for a complicated set of legal rules. If you use the expression without understanding it, you may be in for some unpleasant surprises.

WORK-FOR-HIRE

To understand work-for-hire, let's take a quick look at copyright law. Under copyright law, a creator has a copyright on any writing, music, art, or other creation the moment the work is put into writing or other fixed form, such as a recording, an electronic manuscript, or a software program. The exception to this rule is work-for-hire or work-made-for-hire.

Work-for-hire is owned by the employer or, in some circumstances, the person commissioning the work, and not the original creator. When the creator is an independent freelancer instead of an employee, determining whether the creation is a work-for hire depends on nine criteria, and the Copyright Office publishes a circular on the topic.

Do not assume courts interpret the nine criteria consistently. Courts are as quirky and unpredictable as the people who sit in them. Judges have differing views on what qualifies as "supplemental," "instructional," or "specially ordered."

In California, there is another surprising consequence to calling a project work-for-hire: the freelancer is considered an employee and you are considered the employer unless your freelancer is a corporation, LLC, or other entity. Therefore, you are responsible for unemployment insurance, workers' compensation insurance, and income-tax withholding. This law was passed in response to abuses by software companies, who would hire software developers for months on end, but call them independent contractors to avoid paying additional taxes and providing benefits. As is often the case with laws intended to curb one abuse, they affect the rest of us in unintended ways.

Here is a sample of a general assignment of intellectual property rights:

Effective upon my payment of $_____, you assign and transfer to me the Work Product and all rights, title, and interest in and to the Work Product and all versions, derivatives, and revisions, whether now in existence or to be created in the future, including all copyrights in all languages, in all known or unknown forms, media, or means of expression, all rights to display, perform, reproduce, modify, merchandise, trademark, or otherwise commercially exploit the Work Product. You acknowledge that evolving technology may result in the development of new media and means of expression and exploitation of the Work Product, and agree that this assignment and transfer shall encompass expression and exploitation of the Work Product in all media by all means whether now known or invented in the future.

TAX REPORTING

Remember the Nanny Tax—all the buzz about failing to report payments to babysitters and gardeners that brought down some Presidential appointments? Well, you won't risk public humiliation if you fail to report payments made to editors, cover designers, website designers, publicists, or others, but you could face costly penalties. Plus, you'll pay higher taxes.

General rule: If in any calendar year you pay an independent contractor (other than a corporation) $600 or more for services or $10 or more in royalties in connection with your trade or business, then tax law requires you report those payments on a 1099 MISC and the equivalent state form. Most likely, you are going to pay an editor, cover designer, website designer, and/or publicist $600 or more. Remember, this does not apply to payments to a corporation such as BookBaby, CreateSpace, or Lightning Source.

If you will cross that payment threshold, ask the freelancer for a W-9. The W-9 is a simple form, and it merely verifies the freelancer's Social Security Number or EIN. Then, early in the next calendar year, complete a 1099 MISC, file it with the IRS, and deliver a copy to the freelancer. Don't be intimidated. These are simple forms.

If you report the freelancer's payments on a 1099, then you are in a better position to deduct the expense from your income.

Some freelancers may balk at providing you a W-9 or having you report their payments on a 1099. Perhaps they are not reporting all their income. But to deduct these expenses without raising red flags with the IRS, you must file and deliver 1099s.

ENGAGING FREELANCERS CHECKLIST

- ✓ You have engaged a team of professionals with solid publishing credentials.
- ✓ Editors are polishing your prose.
- ✓ Designers are expanding your vision.
- ✓ All finished work products will be assigned to you.
- ✓ Your publicist is lining up reviews, interviews, and blog tours.
- ✓ You have collected W9s and are ready to send out 1099s.
- ✓ Your author photo captures a confident, accomplished writer, not your bleary-eyed self, staring at the computer screen.
- ✓ You are the master of your own self-publishing universe.

While the bubbly is chilling in anticipation of your book's launch date, let's take a moment to review the ABCs of copyright.

CHAPTER FOUR

GETTING RIGHTS RIGHT

Owning Your Dreams and Creations

Copyrights, fair use, public domain, and licenses; we're getting into the legal thick of it. How do you get a copyright and keep it in effect? What does owning a copyright mean? How do you know if something you find on the Internet is copyrighted or in the public domain? What if you find someone pirating your work? What if someone accuses you of pirating?

Let's refer to two of the CAM guidelines. To **Control** your work and **Avoid** legal entanglements, it helps to understand what you own, what others own, and what no one owns. Knowledge will save you from costly mistakes. Make a cup of tea and read on. You need to know this stuff.

This section focuses on works created after 1978 in the United States.

WHAT EVERY WRITER SHOULD KNOW ABOUT COPYRIGHT

1.   Who owns a copyright?

As soon as you put an idea into a fixed form, whether on a pad of paper, a hard drive, a smartphone, or a recording device, you own the copyright for that creation. Your first draft, riddled with typos, inconsistencies, and clichés, is protected by copyright law whether or not you polish it, publish it, register it, or mark it with a ©. Earlier law required the work to be published and properly marked. If you made an error, you could lose your copyright. Now the copyright attaches easily and automatically.

Everything else about copyrights is complex. Behind every word, even those as ordinary as *original, fixed, publish, display, perform, commission,* or *parody*, there are volumes of legal cases and heated discussions.

2.   What does copyright ownership mean?

A copyright is what is called *intellectual property.* As the owner of a U.S. copyright, you have the exclusive right to

- reproduce the work in books or other forms,
- sell, distribute, and commercially exploit the work,
- create derivative works, such as translations, adaptations, sequels, and abridgements, and
- display or perform the work publicly, either live or in recorded form.

If anyone violates those exclusive rights, you have a claim of *infringement* against the wrongdoer. Of course, there are exceptions. There are always exceptions, and exceptions to the exceptions. The most common is *fair use*, which is discussed later.

3. **What is protected by copyright law?**

Literary works; musical works including lyrics; dramatic works; pictorial, graphic, and sculptural works; sound recordings; architectural works; and pantomimes and choreographic works if fixed in tangible form such as a video recording.

What about characters and settings? Maybe. If a character is as fully developed as Harry Potter or a setting as distinctive as Panem in *The Hunger Games*, the creator might claim copyright protection.

4. **What's NOT protected by copyright law?**

- Titles, names, short phrases, slogans, although you may be able to register these as trademarks, which I'll touch on later,

- Raw data and objective information such as test results and statistics, although the method of organization and any analysis are copyrightable,

- Works not fixed into a tangible form of expression, such as improvisational performances and choreographic works that have not been written or recorded, and

- Ideas, procedures, methods, concepts, principles, and discoveries. A description, explanation, or illustration is copyrightable, but not the underlying concept.

5. **Is © notice required?**

Not technically, but use it anyway. Put it near the front of your book. If your work is properly marked, then an infringer may not claim to be an "innocent infringer," and you may recover a larger award.

The copyright notice has three parts:

1. © or copyright.

2. Year of first publication, which means the year the work was first distributed to the public. On unpublished material, the notice reads "Unpublished Work © year author."

3. Name of copyright owner, which may be a pen name or the name of an entity such as a corporation. If there is more than one copyright owner, name all of them.

If you neglect to put a proper notice on your work, you have five years after the date of publication to fix it.

Also add "All Rights Reserved" because the phrase is required in some foreign countries.

6. Are copyrights transferrable?

Oh, yes. And they are sliced and diced into various pieces.

You may transfer the entire interest in the copyright, which is rarely done. Instead, writers grant *licenses*. A license is a *right to use* only; you, the creator, retain ownership of the copyrighted work. Licenses may be exclusive or nonexclusive, worldwide or geographically restricted, short-term or perpetual, royalty-free or royalty-paying, limited to particular media such as audio books, e-books, print, or a particular language; the permutations are extensive.

A license is similar to a lease. If you are a landlord, you lease portions of your property to various tenants for various periods, but you still own the building. Some apartments may be exclusive to one tenant, meaning only that tenant may use the space. Other portions, such as the lobby, may be used by all the tenants and are nonexclusive. If you grant an exclusive lease or license to more than one person, you are going to have a conflict on your hands.

Exclusive copyright licenses must be in writing, but nonexclusive licenses may be verbal. This makes me shudder; I would hate for someone to publish my work claiming I gave them a verbal, nonexclusive license to do so.

If you grant licenses, be specific about what you are granting. Put everything in writing. It's not to your advantage to use vague descriptions and fuzzy details. Details are your friends. Be redundant, precise, and lawyerly. There is no way to overdo it.

If you are contemplating granting an exclusive license or selling your copyright entirely, study up on licenses and terminology. Or better yet, get an agent or attorney to assist you.

7. Will I ever get back my copyright?

Maybe. A license agreement is ongoing. If the licensee fails to perform as promised, then you may be able to terminate the license. For instance, if your publisher fails to release your book within the time period stated in your contract or fails to pay royalties, you may terminate. But team up with an experienced attorney before you send termination threats.

Under current law, any grant of rights, whether an assignment or license, may be terminable after 35 years. This provision was intended to benefit artists who, for a few dollars, sold creations that went on to be worth millions. The classic example is the case of Jerry Siegel and Joe Shuster, who sold the rights to Superman for $130 in 1940. These artists and their families have fought for decades to regain their rights or a share of the profits. Rock musicians of the 1960s and 1970s are taking advantage of this termination right, or at least threatening to unless paid fair compensation.

While this termination right may exist, its rules are technical, and errors are too easily made. If you are in a position to exercise a termination right, consult an attorney with experience.

8. Is publication required?

Not anymore. However, publication (distribution to the public) is still important.

- The date of publication may determine the duration of the copyright.
- Publication triggers mandatory registration with the Library of Congress. I'll discuss this further under registration.

9. How long will my copyright last?

A copyright created in the United States today lasts for the life of the author plus 70 years. If there are two or more authors, use the life of the last surviving author plus 70 years. The copyright passes to the heirs of the owners, just like any other property interest. If the author is a corporation or other entity, then the copyright lasts 95 years from first publication, but not longer than 120 years after creation of the copyrighted material.

If the copyright was created in the United States before 1977, then the copyright might have expired depending on whether the work was property marked with a copyright notice, when and whether the work was registered, and whether the registration was renewed. Confused? Who isn't? Under Resources, I have a link to a comprehensive chart of copyright expiration dates that is maintained by Cornell University.

10. Should I register my work with the U.S. Copyright Office?

Absolutely. Registration establishes a public, searchable record of your claim and is required before an infringement suit may be filed. Prompt registration (within three months following publication) increases the damages recoverable in an infringement action, plus you may recover attorneys fees. Online registration is currently $35, so there is no excuse for delay. You then mail in two copies of your work.

If you are writing under a pen name, you may register the copyright under the pen name alone (to maintain anonymity), your real name, or both.

You may check the status of your registration online. The process takes up to a year, so do not be surprised if your application shows as INCOMPLETE for months. For assurance that the copies arrived, send them *certified mail, return-receipt requested*.

Many writers do not know they must deposit two copies of their copyrightable work with the Library of Congress within three months following publication. You may satisfy this requirement by registering the work with the Copyright Office and sending the two copies as part of your registration application.

11. Is my copyright international?

Unfortunately, there is no such thing as an international copyright. However, many countries have adopted laws and signed treaties that provide reciprocal recognition of copyrights.

But no law is bulletproof against infringement. If your book is at all successful, then it will be pirated. If the infringers are overseas, there is little you can do without spending an inordinate amount of time and money. Accept a certain level of piracy as part of the business and move on.

12. Will my SPSC or POD company own my copyright?

No, unless they are unscrupulous. When you engage an SPSC, POD provider, or e-book distributor, you will not be and should not be transferring any rights to them other than the nonexclusive right to use your work to produce and distribute books for you, which may include the right to display and market it on their websites.

Never transfer ownership or any exclusive rights to a POD provider or SPSC. Examine your contract for the following terms:

- nonexclusive,

- terminable at any time, and

- after termination, the site retains display and archival copies only.

To help you understand contract provisions to avoid, I will walk you through some key provisions in the Addendum.

Buyers of copies of your book have the nonexclusive license right of *first sale*, which means they may resell, trade, or give away their copy. They may not copy, perform, or create derivative works based on your book, unless their actions fall within the fair use exception.

ARE BOOK TITLES PROTECTED BY COPYRIGHT LAW?

Not usually. Anyone who has written a novel will tell you how difficult it is to come up with a title that is resonant and eye-catching, so it is ironic that titles are not protected because they are considered too short to contain sufficient "original expression."

But there may be a way to protect your book title: trademark law. Not all titles will qualify as trademarks; your title must satisfy the following criteria.

Your title must be unique and distinctive. Go on Amazon and search betrayed. You'll find over 25 books with that title. If your title consists solely of one or more common words, then you can write off claiming it as a trademark, with one exception that I'll discuss below. For trademark purposes, the best titles are unique, made-up words like *Swamplandia* or *Freakonomics*.

Your title must be more than merely descriptive. Purely descriptive titles, such as Hiking Trails of the Sierras or How to Trim an Apple Tree, are rarely trademarks.

Your title has become well-known. Even if you have a common or a descriptive title, all is not lost. If your book is so successful that consumers associate the title primarily with your book, then the title has achieved "secondary meaning" and might be considered a common law trademark. The *Twilight* Series is a perfect example.

Your book is part of a series. You are more likely to gain trademark status for the name of a series of books, such as *Harry Potter, Diary of a Wimpy Kid,* and the *For Dummies* line.

Your title is part of a broader business venture. If your book grew out of (or grows into) a larger enterprise such as consulting, public speaking, workshops, DVD sales, or merchandising, then your title and related phrases are trademarks (for example, *Freakonomics*).

FAIR USE

Owning a copyrighted work gives you **control** over who may use your work and how, but only up to a point. You cannot prohibit someone from using portions of the work for criticism, no matter how scathing. You may have to tolerate parody even if it is offensive and distasteful. The First Amendment protects these forms of speech as *fair use* even when they incorporate your copyrighted work.

Fair use is defined as any copying of copyrighted material (even verbatim) for a limited or *"transformative"* purpose, such as commentary, criticism, or parody. Such uses may be done without permission from the copyright owner.

The line between fair use and infringement is murky. Much depends on the facts of the case, the aggressiveness of the copyright owner, and the temperament of the judge.

There is no specific number of words that may be used without permission. The old 300-*word* rule was an unspoken agreement among publishers, not the law. Noncommercial or educational use is not 100 percent safe, particularly if you use a substantial part of the original material. Giving credit to the author does not make a difference—you could be infringing even if you are not plagiarizing.

By law, courts take four factors into consideration when weighing fair use. No one factor controls.

1. The purpose and character of the alleged fair use.

- Is the use commercial or for nonprofit, newsworthy, or educational purposes?
- Does the new work offer something more than the original? The buzzword is *transformative*. If the work is altered significantly, used for a new purpose, and/or modified to appeal to a different audience, then it is more likely to be fair use.

2. The nature of the original work.

- Is the copyrighted work a published or unpublished work? Using unpublished works is less likely to be fair use because of factor number four—potential adverse effect on the value of the original work.
- Is the original work out of print? Traditionally, this favored a fair-use determination due to the public interest of keeping important works available for discussion. With the technology to revive out-of-print books as e-books, this distinction is no longer meaningful.
- Is the original work factual or artistic? Reusing factual content is more likely to be fair use, while reusing artistic elements is not.

3. **The amount and substantiality of the portion used in relation to the original work as a whole.**

   • The more you use, the less likely the use will be considered fair use, especially if you incorporate the *heart* or *essence* of the original work.

4. **The effect of the use upon the potential market for, or value of, the original work.**

   • Is the use likely to affect the copyright owner's economic gain? The more adverse the effect, the less likely the use will be deemed fair use.

Fair use applies only to copyrighted work. The portions of any work not subject to copyright—titles, historical facts, data, test results, ideas, and concepts—may be used regardless of any fair use standard.

Generally, the following are considered fair use:

   • quotations or excerpts in a review, or scholarly or technical work for purposes of illustration or comment,
   • parody,
   • summaries, with brief quotations, in a news report, and
   • reproduction by a teacher or student of a small part of a work to illustrate a lesson.

Here are some examples of uses that were *not* fair use:

   • a book of trivia questions based upon the *Seinfeld* TV show,
   • a *Harry Potter* Encyclopedia,
   • a news program showing one minute and fifteen seconds of the Rodney King beating. In contrast, the use of still images and clips from Abraham Zapruder's film of JFK's assassination are frequently considered fair use due to their newsworthy nature, and

- a parody of the O.J. Simpson trial based on *The Cat in the Hat* by Dr. Seuss, because it used the book to parody an unrelated event. In contrast, 2 Live Crew's rap-style rewrite of Roy Orbison's *Oh, Pretty Woman* was held to be a parody and fair use because it poked fun at the song itself.

To confuse matters, there's the new Google ruling. The U.S. Circuit Court in New York has ruled that Google's scanning of over 20 billion books and permitting its users to view excerpts of them constitutes fair use because it provides a public benefit without adversely affecting the rights of copyright holders. The Authors Guild and others disagree, and the case is being appealed.

If you think these distinctions seem contrived, you are correct. Court rulings on fair use are inconsistent and frequently contradictory.

The safest course is to get permission from the copyright owner. Do not rely on fair use except for those cases when it appears to be most obvious and supportable. Even if you are well within safe lines, the copyright owner might sue. Fair use is a defense, which means if you are sued for infringement, then you have the burden of proving that your use fits within the fair use exception. Think of the attorneys' fees and the time involved. While I admire those who take on David-and-Goliath battles, I'd rather spend my time and energy writing my next book.

PUBLIC DOMAIN

True or False: If an image, poem, essay, or short story is posted on the Internet, it is in the public domain and anyone may use it.

False, but many people seem to forget this, especially when it applies to images. There are five major categories of public domain works.

1. **Works where the copyright has expired.** For example, Shakespeare's plays, Mozart's sonatas, and your own photograph of Leonardo da Vinci's *Mona Lisa*. For works created and copyrighted in the United States, any work first published prior to January 1, 1923 is in the public domain. This includes some early silent films and blues recordings. If the work was created prior to 1977, the copyright may have expired if the work was not properly marked or registered, or if its registration was not renewed. The duration of copyrights for works created in different countries may be different.

2. **Works where the copyright was lost.** Typically, copyright claims were lost if the work was published without the proper notice prior to March 1, 1989.

3. **Works created by the U.S. federal government.** Take a look at the tens of millions of images, recordings, personal narratives, reports, and other works that are available on the Library of Congress website. I list other government sites under Resources.

4. **Works that are not copyrightable.** As I discussed above, some works such as ideas, procedures, methods, concepts, principles, book titles, raw data, and objective information are not protected by copyright and so are in the public domain.

5. **Works donated to the public domain through a Creative Commons license.** A creator may use the Creative Commons CC0 mark to designate a work that has been donated to the public domain. The Creative Commons has a similar mark for works already in the public domain.

GETTING PERMISSIONS

By now, you have internalized the warnings: don't use content plucked off the Internet without permission. Suppose you find an image, lyrics, or a song you want to use; how do you find the copyright owner and obtain permission?

The Internet has simplified searching for a copyright owner of a work created in the last 35 years. However, even if you discover who created a work, identifying who has the right to grant you permission may be more difficult. The original creator may have sold its rights, which may have then been resold a dozen times. A corporate owner may have changed its name or merged with another company.

If the writing, song, lyric, art, or other copyrightable work was first published on or after January 1, 1923, do a diligent search. Write down where you searched and what you found. Keep the list in case you ever have to show you made a good-faith effort to identify the copyright owner.

Start with the website of the U.S. Copyright Office. Their online records go back as far as 1978 and include books, music, films, sound recordings, maps, photographs, art periodicals, and newspapers. You can also have the Copyright Office conduct a search for you. Current rate is $200 per hour.

Columbia University Libraries provides additional search tools, particularly for musical, dramatic, and sculptural works. Google Books also provides a search portal. Stanford University maintains a database of renewals, which is especially helpful if you are trying to determine if an older work (pre-1964) renewed its registration and received the benefit of the 95-year copyright term. The University of Pennsylvania also provides links to historic registration records.

For international searches, the University of Cambridge provides some helpful resources.

For fine art, try the Visual Artists Gallery Association (VAGA), Artists Rights Society (ARS), or Graphic Arts Guide. For comics, try Comicon.

Commercial services, such as Copyright Clearance Center (CCC) and Publication Rights Clearinghouse (PRC) will also assist you in obtaining licenses and permissions.

Links to these various sites can be found under Resources at the end of the Handbook and on my website. Also check out my ebooks HOW TO USE EYE-CATCHING IMAGES WITHOUT PAYING A FORTUNE OR A LAWYER and HOW TO USE MEMORABLE LYRICS WITHOUT PAYING A FORTUNE OR A LAWYER (to be released late 2014).

STOCK IMAGES AND MUSIC

If you cannot obtain permission to use an image, you could hire an illustrator or designer to prepare a custom image for you. That's the Cadillac solution. The VW version is to purchase stock images.

Millions of photographs, illustrations, and vector images are available at online sites such as Dreamstime, Fotolia, Shutterstock, IStockPhoto, Getty Images, and Time Life Photos. For celebrity photos, try Corbis Images. The images are high quality and reasonably priced. Prices range from $1 to thousands of dollars, but my guess is 95 percent of the images cost less than $100. Images are available in different sizes and DPI (dots per inch, a measure of resolution quality). The higher the DPI, the better the clarity and resolution of the image. For your book cover, purchase a license to a large, high-resolution image, but for your website and blog an image with a lower resolution may work fine.

Many of these sites also have music clips and videos. I created the book trailer for *Coyote Winds* using stock images and music licensed from Dreamstime and iStockPhoto for under $150.

Purchase a *royalty-free license* and *not* an *editorial license*, which has more restrictions on use. A license means permission to use. You are not buying the copyright or ownership to the image, but the "perpetual, nonexclusive, nontransferable, nonsublicensable, world-right to reproduce the image," subject to some limitations I describe below. Royalty-free is a misnomer; you are paying the royalty up-front.

Nonexclusive means others may have the right to use the image as well. For exclusive rights (if available), the sites will charge extra, but they cannot do anything about rights already granted. Many illustrators and photographers post their work on multiple sites, so buying exclusive rights from one site may not stop sales on other sites.

The site iStockPhoto lists the following permitted uses for royalty-free licensed images, which are fairly typical:

- books and book covers, magazines, newspapers, editorials, newsletters; and video, broadcast and theatrical presentations and other entertainment applications,

- advertising and promotional projects, including printed materials, product packaging, presentations, film and video presentations, commercials, catalogues, brochures, promotional greeting cards, and promotional postcards (i.e., not for resale or license),

- online or electronic publications, and

- prints, posters, and other reproductions for personal use or promotional purposes, but not for resale, license, or other distribution.

The typical off-the-shelf license has some limitations, although you can purchase expanded rights for additional fees. You may **not** use the licensed image:

- as part of a trademark or logo,
- as part of a design-template application intended for resale, such as website templates, business-card templates, electronic greeting-card templates, or "on demand" products, such as postcards, mugs, T-shirts, and hats (you can create T-shirts and such for promotional uses, but not for sale),
- in a manner that is pornographic, obscene, immoral, infringing, defamatory or libelous, or that would be reasonably likely to bring any person or property reflected in the image into disrepute; or be in any way unflattering or offensive. Use your common sense here. If you would not want a picture of you, your sister, your mother, or your child manipulated a certain way, then don't do it, and
- in any manner that looks as if the model or person is endorsing the product, unless you say it is a model.

Some sites permit you to use the image an unlimited number of times. Others set a limit of 249,999 or 499,999 printed images and unlimited Internet images. If you distribute over 249,999 printed copies of your book, bookmarks, postcards, and other materials, then you need to buy an extended license. I hope every reader of this book has that problem!

You cannot sell, transfer, or permit someone else to use the licensed image, other than someone you hire to use the image for your benefit, such as a website designer or cover designer.

Be careful about using stock images on social media sites. Even if you pay for a license, if you post that image on Facebook, and then Facebook turns around and uses that image in its advertising, your license could be *terminated*. Honestly, I do not know how this will be monitored and enforced, especially since social media sites frequently change their privacy and reposting rules. But it is part of the typical stock image license.

Getty Images recently announced it was making over 35 million images available for free for editorial, noncommercial purposes, with strings attached. The images must be imbedded, which means they will appear with the Getty logo and other advertising content. Also, Getty may remove the photo from your site at any time, so I would not rely upon these *free* images for anything important.

HOW TO SCRUB ILLEGAL IMAGES FROM YOUR WEBSITE

Everyone does it. Downloads a great image from a blog or news site, pastes it on their own blog, and moves on, forgetting, ignoring, or not knowing they are using someone else's property without permission. Every day, your chances of getting caught escalate. You will open your email one morning to find a nasty lawyer letter demanding a thousand-dollar payment.

Reverse-image search engines are expanding their reach. Casual photographers to international stock-image companies is signing up with TinEye and others to scan the Internet for infringing users. TinEye claims to have indexed over four billion images.

What about fair use? Maybe you are using the image for noncommercial or educational purposes. You may be right, but do you want to fight that fight with Getty Images or Rupert Murdoch? Wouldn't it be easier to clean up your blog? Here's how.

First, determine who owns an image. You can search for an image, just as you search for a word, by using reverse-image search engines. Go to TinEye or Google Images and upload the image. On

Google Images, click on the camera icon in the search line and upload the image you want searched. You will get a list of results.

If you discover the image is licensed by one or more stock image sites, then you face a good chance of getting caught. These companies actively troll the Internet. I suggest you either delete the image or buy a license to use it from one of these stock-images sites ASAP. (If it's one of Getty's free images, then imbed it as Getty instructs on its website.) Replace the image on your blog with the licensed or imbedded image, and keep your receipt. You might get a demand letter based upon your use prior to buying the license, but it will help if you have corrected the mistake.

If you find the image on news sites, look for a copyright notice on or near the image. If you can't find a copyright notice, contact the largest and most prestigious website using the image. That site is most likely to have obtained the required permissions. Then contact the owner and ask permission to use the image.

If you cannot determine who owns the image, or cannot get permission, or do not want to pay for the license—or if all this is too much bother for you—then replace the image with something in the public domain or a free image under the appropriate Creative Commons license.

CREATIVE COMMONS: A BLOGGER'S GOLD MINE

Creative Commons is one of the best innovations to grow out of global interconnectivity.

Under copyright law, for a copyright holder to grant others, such as publishers and filmmakers, the right to use copyrighted materials, licenses are granted on a one-by-one basis. Traditional copyright law does not provide a practical way to permit wide-ranging use of copyrighted work.

Creative Commons is a non-profit organization that has developed a set of off-the-shelf licenses for use by copyright holders who wish to make their work widely available for limited or unlimited purposes. To quote the Creative Commons website, "Our tools give everyone from individual creators to large companies and institutions a simple, standardized way to grant copyright permissions to their creative work."

There are currently six basic Creative Commons licenses, each with its own icon, set of rights, and limitations.

- Attribution
- Attribution-No Derivatives
- Attribution-ShareAlike
- Attribution-NonCommercial
- Attribution-NonCommercial-Share Alike
- Attribution-NonCommercial-No Derivatives

Creative Commons also provides an icon for designating that a work has been donated to the public domain with "No Rights Reserved."

The Creative Commons site provides both "human" explanations of their licenses as well as full "legalese" versions. For example, here is a portion of their "human" (as opposed to legalese) **Attribution-NonCommercial/ShareAlike License:**

YOU ARE FREE

- *to share*—to copy, distribute and transmit the work.
- *to remix*—to adapt
- the work.
- *under the following conditions:*

- *Attribution*—You must attribute the work in the manner specified by the author or licensor (but not in any way that suggests that they endorse you or your use of the work).
- *Noncommercial*—You may not use this work for commercial purposes.
- *ShareAlike*—If you alter, transform, or build upon this work, you may distribute the resulting work only under the same or similar license to this one.

HOW DO WRITERS USE CREATIVE COMMONS LICENSES?

As the Licensor: To put the world on notice that a certain expression, let's say your blog, is available for copying and modification, mark your blog with the appropriate Creative Commons mark. The Creative Commons site has a simple questionnaire to help you determine the correct license. For example, Wikipedia uses the Creative Commons Attribution-ShareAlike License.

As a Licensee: If you are searching for images, content, or other expression for your use, the Creative Commons site provides links to some of the larger databases for images and other content, including Flickr, Al Jezeera, Wikipedia, and the White House. Google Images has a tool for sorting images by usage rights. Since there are various Creative Commons licenses that provide different permissions, look at the icons carefully and read what is or is not permitted. Choose the license that covers all your intended uses, such as commercial and derivative. Your blog may be primarily informative and educational, but if you also provide links to Amazon or other sellers of your book, your use may be considered commercial. You'll always want to provide attribution to the creator of the content you're using. The Creative Commons site provides guidelines.

One warning about using Creative Commons images containing people or featuring another copyrighted work, such as a painting, poster, or sculpture: You have no reliable way of determining whether the photographer obtained releases from the people in the image or permission to use the underlying art. Do not rely on the Creative Commons license if there are recognizable faces or artwork in the image.

If you want to use an image showing a person, then create your own (with the appropriate releases) or purchase a stock image from one of the larger companies. They provide an assurance that the appropriate releases and permissions were obtained (and, in addition, they have deeper pockets to pay for lawsuits should they be wrong).

FAN FICTION: A STUDY IN FAIR USE

Fan fiction uses characters and settings from popular books, movies, and television shows, and puts them in new situations and adventures. *Star Trek*, *Harry Potter*, *Buffy the Vampire Slayer*, and *Twilight* have all spawned countless fan-fiction works. Writers have created prequels, sequels, alternative endings, and mixed-up romantic pairings.

However, fan fiction is legally problematic. Since it relies on characters and settings created by others, fan fiction may be considered derivative work that infringes on the original source material. Others claim fan fiction is transformative and therefore fair use.

If you are publishing fan fiction for commercial purposes, you are entering risky territory. Use as little of the original work as possible and add new, transformative elements. Insert a disclaimer stating your fan-fiction piece was NOT created by the original author, but give the original author credit.

Many authors and producers encourage fan fiction because it increases exposure of the underlying work. Others tolerate it as long as it is not obscene or offensive. But some are quick to set their lawyers loose on fan-fiction writers. Don't be one of those writers.

I would not invest a lot of creative energy into a commercial project before researching whether the owner of the underlying work encourages fan fiction or squelches it. Some will grant licenses for fan-fiction projects if requested. I highly recommend getting a license if it is available. Even if your creation is brilliantly transformative and clearly fair use, publishing and film companies hire big-time lawyers to make your life miserable. As I have said before, stay out of court and at your desk writing your next book.

Enter Amazon. Amazon has jumped into the fan-fiction phenomenon. It has licensed several popular works and created a publishing platform for commercializing fan fiction on Kindle, called Kindle Worlds. The licensed works include *Gossip Girl* by Cecily von Ziegesar, *Pretty Little Liars* by Sara Shepard, and *The Vampire Diaries* by L.J. Smith.

Before publishing fan fiction on Kindle Worlds, read the publishing agreement carefully. If you agree, then you will be granting to Amazon "an exclusive, irrevocable license for the full term of copyright (including renewals), to develop, license, reproduce, print, publish, distribute, translate, display, publicly perform and transmit your work, in whole and in part, in each country in the world, in all languages and formats, and by all means now known or later developed, and the right to prepare derivative works of your work."

Ouch! This is a 180-degrees departure from the CreateSpace or KDP agreements, which did not claim such broad or long-lasting rights in your work. In addition, the royalty rates for Kindle Worlds' books are lower than the royalties paid on books distributed through

CreateSpace and KDP. I suspect the owners of the underlying works have dictated these terms.

What if your work becomes the target of fan fiction?

You have two choices. Sit back and enjoy the ride. The publicity may boost sales. Or fight it, in which case read *Chapter Ten: Attorneys.*

PROTECTING IDEAS

Many artists and writers are distressed to hear that ideas are not protected by copyright. After all, aren't ideas the core of a creative work and the spark most worth protecting?

Think about it. How many times have you had what seemed like a brilliant idea, but when you sat down to turn it into a book, the idea sputtered out around page 30, or page 5, or page 2? An idea has little value unless you craft it into something more. It's the execution of the idea that is valuable and protectable.

If you want to protect your ideas and have some additional protection for your manuscript, you could ask agents, editors, and other freelancers to sign a Non-Disclosure Agreement (NDA).

Most agents and publishers will flat out refuse to sign. I doubt they are planning on stealing your ideas, but they may already be working on something similar and fear you will accuse them of stealing.

In fact, they may send you an agreement that looks something like this: *Agent and/or any of its clients may have created, may create, or may otherwise have access to materials, ideas, and creative works which may be similar or identical to your material with regard to theme, motif, plots, characters, formats, or other attributes; and you shall not be entitled to any compensation because of the proposed use or use of any such similar or identical material.*

For freelancers you hire, asking for an NDA is reasonable. However, if you are talking about your project on your blog or writers' forums, you can't expect your freelancer to be bound to keep confidential what you have already made public. I posted a form of NDA on my blog.

DRM: A SURPRISING CONTROVERSY

DRM, short for *digital rights management,* stands for any software or hardware device that deters unauthorized copying or viewing of content, such as e-books, music, and film. It is the lock and key for digital copyrighted material. Any digital file downloaded without DRM is easily copied.

If you publish your e-book through KDP, then you have the option of adding DRM to your work. But SmashWords and other e-book publishers and distributors will not accept e-books with DRM. Surprised? I was.

DRM is controversial. You wouldn't think so. You work months or years on a book. Of course, you put a lock on it to protect it against unauthorized copying and piracy. You lock your home and your car—why not your *intellectual property?*

Mark Coker, founder of SmashWords, explained his reasons for discouraging DRM:

- **Printed books never die.** They are lent to friends, donated to libraries, and sold as used books, and no one calls that piracy. Why impose tighter restrictions on e-books?
- **"Obscurity is a bigger threat to authors than piracy."** I heard Mark say these words at a conference, and despite my dreams of being a *New York Times* best-selling author, I have to admit he is correct. I have given away hundreds of books intentionally, so maybe a few more are being given away unintentionally. The more people read my book, the more likely word-of-mouth will spread. And let's face it, word-of-mouth sells books.

- **The vast majority of readers are willing to pay a fair price for a good read.** True, so far. I wonder how long that will last as we grow more accustomed to obtaining reading material on the Internet for free.

- **DRM doesn't work.** Remember when the music industry tried to control unauthorized downloads by adding DRM? Remember people getting arrested? Well, that blew up in the face of the music industry as more people began to download music illegally out of spite, and software geeks proved getting around DRM was a piece of cake. DRM doesn't stop the crooks. Of course, people say the same about locking one's house, but I still do it.

By the way, you do not need DRM to protect your copyright. Some people worry that not applying DRM to their intellectual property is equivalent to donating their work to the public domain. Legally speaking, no. You still own the copyright. But I recommend authors put a copyright notice and "All Rights Reserved" near the front of their e-books to put the world on notice of ownership.

GETTING RIGHTS RIGHT CHECKLIST

After reading this chapter, you have a better understanding of the bundle of rights known as copyright, including

- ✓ how a copyright is created, licensed, and protected,
- ✓ why it's important to register your copyright within three months following the release of your book,
- ✓ what constitutes fair use,
- ✓ how to identify works in the public domain,
- ✓ when to ask permission to use the work of others,
- ✓ how to find a copyright holder,

✓ how to find images, music, and other content for little or
   no money, and

✓ the pros and cons of DRM.

You may even be tempted to try your hand at fan fiction.

Now that you are armed with a better understanding of the
scope and limitations of intellectual property rights, let's get back to
the business issues of producing, marketing, and distributing your
book. It's time to share your creation with the world.

CHAPTER FIVE

MARKETING AND DISTRIBUTION

Getting the Attention You Deserve

After you have your manuscript edited and designed, it is time to build your readership. This is a two-step process. First, readers must be aware your book is available and worth reading. Second, you must place the book in their hands either as an e-book or print book.

Since you will not have a traditional publishing company lining up reviews, scheduling interviews, and placing advertisements on your behalf, you will be your own marketing director. If you are working with an SPSC, your package may include some marketing services such as promotional copy and prepaid *Kirkus* and *Clarion* reviews. Even with these services, 99 percent of the marketing work falls on your shoulders.

If you search "how to promote your book" online, you'll find hundreds of websites and blog posts offering suggestions. With thousands following the same advice, how do you stand out in the crowd?

One writer, Jennifer Belle, hired actresses to read her book in public and laugh out loud. The stunt got her coverage in the New York Times and the New York Post, radio talk-show interviews, and coverage in blogs. She sold books and generated buzz.

The most outrageous stunt must be the German publisher Eichborn (their logo looks like a fly) attaching tiny banners printed with their logo to hundreds of flies and releasing them at the 2009 Frankfurt Book Fair. This video is worth watching.

http://www.mhpbooks.com/winner-of-most-bizarre-publicity-stunt-award-revealed/

Your mailbox will be flooded with offers for products or services that will claim to sell thousands of books, launch your book to the top of Amazon's rankings, and let you quit your day job. Some are outright scams, but most are myths: great ideas that don't work. In marketing, there are no miracles—only hard work and luck. You have to plant a lot of seeds and hope at least one of them grows into a tree.

CREATING A MARKETING PLAN

Make a marketing plan to organize your efforts. Start by identifying your target reader. Intense marketing to a niche group is far more effective than diluted marketing to the entire world. Trying to sell romance books to nonfiction readers is a waste of resources. Advertising your dog-training book on a bodybuilding site is inefficient. Focus on the blogs, publications, websites, and conferences most likely to reach your readers.

Consider engaging a publicist for the months leading up to and immediately following your launch. A good publicist has contacts with editors, interviewers, reviewers, bookstores, and other potential sources of exposure that you'll never have. Choose a publicist with experience and contacts in your niche. The more focused, the better.

A social-media consultant is another valuable team member, who can help educate you and get you started using Twitter, Pinterest, Google Plus, and time-saving apps like HootSuite, Twylah, SocialOomph, and Social Report. Many are experts on *branding*, which, despite its sound, has nothing to do with cattle (although a lot to do with herding).

Like writing, marketing is an open-ended, potentially never-ending task. Mark an end date on your calendar, so you will know when to scale back on marketing and move on to your next project.

The legal issues fall into three categories:

- avoiding deceptive marketing practices,
- understanding your distribution options and limitations, and
- identifying scams and myths.

REVIEWS AND SOCK-PUPPETRY

Nothing sells books better than five-star reviews. They are word-of-mouth recommendations on steroids. They increase visibility on Amazon's search engine, generate blog posts and interviews, and boost credibility. Good reviews beget more good reviews.

So it is not surprising that five-star reviews are being manipulated and monetized.

No doubt you have heard about *sock-puppetry*—authors posting reviews, comments, and tweets under fake names. But that is small potatoes.

Paid reviews have become a big business. The *New York Times* reported on a site called GettingBooksReviewed.com, which offered 50 positive reviews for $999. The website owner was pulling in $28,000 a month, and the reviewers were not even reading the books. The news story generated so much backlash that the website shut down, and Amazon deleted all the paid-for reviews it could identify. These services still exist. I recently found one, Paidbookreviews.org. It offers five reviews for $125 and 1,000 reviews for $2,400.

Industry book-review magazines like *Kirkus Reviews* and *Fore-Word Reviews* charge up to $575 for a single review, although their reviewers actually read the book.

On a smaller scale, sites such as StoryCartel.com connect readers and authors by offering free e-books in exchange for honest reviews. Thousands of bloggers review books if they receive them for free. Then there are peer reviews where authors trade reviews of one another's books.

Do paid, solicited, or bartered reviews compromise the integrity of the system? Is all this honest, ethical, legal? Let's look at legality.

On the federal level, the Federal Trade Commission has rules regarding endorsements, and a review may be considered an endorsement. Endorsers may be liable for civil penalties if (i) they make false or unsubstantiated claims about a product or service, or (ii) fail to disclose a *material* connection with the product or service.

Posting a review of your own book would be a material connection, as would posting a review for a family member or friend, and technically the connection should be disclosed.

However, the risk of incurring penalties is low. To date, the FTC has pursued few violators and only for egregious violations. One was a public relations firm that posted hundreds of positive reviews under false names for its clients. To be on the safe side, many bloggers disclose when they have received free books or swag from authors they are reviewing. However, I do not know of anyone disclosing that their reviews are from friends and family.

On the state level, most states have laws prohibiting misleading advertising or marketing practices, and a bogus review could be considered misleading. Along with other lawyers, I question how much consumers are truly misled by reviews, no matter how disingenuous. The manipulation of reviews is widespread, and not just on Amazon. Some of the worst transgressions have been on sites such as TripAdvisor and Yelp. Sony Corporation has been accused of creating a fictitious film critic to post reviews. John Mackey, the CEO of Whole Foods, was accused of using a false identity to post comments on Yahoo Finance. Some bogus reviewers have gone to jail, but only when the reviews were part of a larger fraud.

Regardless of the law, posting bogus reviews raises questions about ethics and trust. As I mentioned before, readers expect you to deal with them honestly even if you are selling a book about how to rob a bank or hack the Pentagon. Lose their trust and you lose the readers.

What is an independent author to do? It's unavoidable. As a self-published author, you are going to have to pay money and give away books to get reviews, at least at first. But there are better and worse approaches.

For me, the deciding factor is transparency. I see no problem with buying and posting a review from *Kirkus* or *ForeWord* or offering a free e-book in exchange for a review on StoryCartel, as long as that information is known or available to anyone reading the review.

(By the way, no amount of money will buy an independent author a review in *The New York Times*, *The New York Review of Books*, or the *Los Angeles Times*.)

PAID REVIEW SERVICES

Certain industry book-review magazines have gone into the business of reviewing indie books at a steep price. These reviews are considered legitimate, and you may post excerpts on Amazon, your website, and in your book, subject to some rules imposed by each site. The quality of the reviews ranges from a high-school book report to a thoughtful essay. The magazines do not guarantee a favorable review, although some will permit you to make an unfavorable review disappear. You have to pay your money and take your chances.

As of March 2014, the larger sites and their prices are as follows:

- *Kirkus Reviews.* For a review of 250-300 words, $425 for standard turnaround of seven to nine weeks; $575 for expedited turnaround of four to six weeks.

- *ForeWord Reviews.* For a review of 450 words, $499 for four-to-six week turnaround. If they determine your book is high quality and you have submitted it at least three months prior to its publication date, they may review it for free.

- *Midwest Book Review.* No fees (unless you are sending an e-book or unpublished manuscript; then the fee is $50). Not all submitted books are reviewed. Long turnaround time, 14 to 16 weeks.

- *BlueInk Review.* $395 for seven-to-nine-week turnaround; $495 for four-to-five-week turnaround.

The following book-review sites are independent of a publication and are relatively new:

- Compulsion Reads.com. The price for a review of 300-400 words depends on the length of the work. For an 80,000-

word book, the price is $79.99. Four-to-six-week turna-
round.

- YourFirstReview.com. For a review of 300 words, $149.
  Five-to-seven-business-day turnaround.

- PacificBookReview.com. Various packages include a review
  of 400-600 words, posting of the review on retail sites, press
  releases, and additional promotional materials. Prices range
  from $299 to $495, and the turnaround is three weeks.

- SelfPublishingReview.com. For a review of 500 words, prices
  start at $109. Two-to-eight-week turnaround.

This list is not complete. More sites offering paid reviews are
launching every month.

REVIEWS BY BLOGGERS

Thousands of bloggers will review books if they meet certain criteria. Search for bloggers who cover your genre and have a significant
following. Before approaching the blogger, read the blog's review
policies. Some will not accept self-published books. Others are particular about what they will read.

The best of these bloggers post their reviews on their blog and
also on Amazon, Barnes & Noble.com, and Goodreads, even if they
are negative. Unlike *Kirkus* and *ForeWord*, bloggers are unlikely to
delete a negative review.

Good publicists and social-media consultants connect you with
bloggers. I have seen advertisements for companies that canvas bloggers
for you and claim to have a list of bloggers waiting to read and review
your book—for a price. These services would save you hours, but I do
not know whether they generate any sales.

If you review books on your blog, I recommend you disclose in a
"clear and conspicuous manner" whether you received the book for

free and whether you will receive a commission on any sale made through your site, such as through an affiliate program. No special lawyer-language is needed. Plain English will work.

AMAZON VINE AND TOP REVIEWERS

Amazon offers publishers the opportunity to put their products before Amazon's Vine Voices, who are recruited from the site's most active and trusted reviewers. These reviewers are provided free products, including books, in exchange for reviews. The program has been criticized because it elevates nonprofessional reviewers (and their reviews) above the reviews of legitimate reviewers.

Some authors approach Amazon's Top Reviewers and Hall of Fame Reviewers directly. They email several hundred with a pitch and find a dozen reviewers willing to look at their work, *maybe*. I have seen ads for companies—similar to the blogging services—that will search and contact Amazon Top Reviewers for you. Otherwise, you have to do the legwork yourself.

Amazon and retail sites have their own rules regarding reviews. Amazon will remove any review it believes is paid-for or was posted by a related party. I know of authors who have had reviews deleted when Amazon identified five-star reviews that have been traded between authors. If Amazon eliminates a review in error, they may be receptive to reposting the review if you contact them and support your claim that the review is legitimate.

UNPAID BUT SOLICITED REVIEWS

Other sources for reviews are your friends, neighbors, family, and fellow writers. I see no problem with giving free books to those you know and asking for a review, as long as you couch the request with, "If you like the book, I'd sure appreciate a review."

Prepare yourself. I find that for every five people who say they will write a review, maybe one comes through. Maybe.

UNPAID AND UNSOLICITED REVIEWS

The reviews with the most integrity are those you receive from legitimate buyers of your book. Nothing feels sweeter than receiving a glowing review from a stranger. Knowing you touched a reader enough for her to write a five-star review makes all the work and expense of writing and self-publishing worthwhile.

THE POWER OF AMAZON RANKING

Once your book is released, you will find yourself checking your book's Amazon sales ranking far too often. It's listed under Product Details as Amazon's Best Sellers Rank.

Ranking is highly volatile. The sale of one paperback may boost the book's ranking from 1,100,000 to 110,000, at least for a short time. The rankings are updated hourly.

Amazon is secretive about their methods for determining ranking. Teresa Ragan, a self-published author who has enjoyed best-selling success, posted her analysis of Amazon rankings on her website, http://www.theresaragan.com/

An Amazon Ranking of:

- 50,000 to 100,000 indicates sales of one copy per day.
- 10,000 to 50,000 indicates sales of 5 to 15 copies per day.
- 3,000 to 10,000 indicates sales of 15 to 70 copies per day.
- 750 to 3,000 indicates sales of 70 to 120 copies per day.
- 350 to 750 indicates sales of 120 to 250 copies per day.
- 200 to 350 indicates sales of 250 to 500 copies per day.
- 35 to 200 indicates sales of 500 to 2,000 copies per day.

- 20 to 35 indicates sales of 2,000 to 3,000 copies per day.
- 5 to 20 indicates sales of 3,000 to 4,000 copies per day.
- 1 to 5 indicates sales of 4,000+ copies per day.

Amazon has over 4,000,000 titles. If you have a ranking under 10,000 (about 15 copies per day), then you are doing very well.

ADVERTISING

It goes without saying that your advertisements must be truthful. Don't claim awards you have not won or make up blurbs from famous writers. Don't laugh; this happens.

Advertising opportunities are so vast I cannot address them here except to give guidance on what to look for when spending your advertising dollars.

First, before you commit to an advertising buy, try to determine if the channel is effective. Contact authors advertising on the site or publication. Check their sales rankings on Amazon. If the rankings are dismal, take that as a warning. I considered advertising in the Independent Press Listing of the *New York Review of Books.* The prestige of the publication intrigued me. When I scanned the Amazon rankings of the books being advertised, many were down in the depths of one to three millionth. I passed.

Most websites and search engines bill you by the "click through." You are charged only when someone clicks on your link. Look for sites that target ads to specific audiences. Focus your efforts to your most likely readers. Start with small packages (25 to 100 clicks). See which sites and advertisements generate more clicks. If you are pre-paying for a set number of clicks, ask if the site will refund any unused payment.

Advertising rates are highly negotiable. Communicate with the sales staff directly. You are likely to get a substantial discount off the publicized "rack rate."If you are committing significant money, do so only with well-established sites and publications. If the venue goes under, you are unlikely to see your money again.

As always, read your contract. If the salesperson makes promises, make sure those promises are captured in writing.

E-BLASTS AND NEWSLETTERS

Email announcements or blasts (known as *e-blasts*) are the modern version of junk mail. You can purchase mailing lists focused on a particular market—such as middle school history teachers, personal trainers for seniors, or chinchilla owners—from companies such as ListGIANT. You could build one yourself using your contacts on Twitter, LinkedIn, and other sites.

Try aligning your book with a cause, and ask charitable organizations to promote your book to their members in return for a percentage of sales. With email and direct-mail campaigns, prepare yourself for a low response rate. A one- to two-percent response rate is considered successful.

Email blasts and newsletters are SPAM, even if you are emailing people who have opted into receiving your material. If you send them using your standard email box, your email address and perhaps your domain may be shut down by your ISP for being a spammer. Use a service such as MailChimp or Constant Contact to send out bulk emails and newsletters. Not only do they provide the opt-out service required with SPAM, they include helpful analytics.

DISTRIBUTION OF PRINT BOOKS

I dreamed my book, *Coyote Winds*, was featured in the window of the Barnes & Noble at 82nd and Broadway in Manhattan, the store closest to where I grew up. Old friends and neighbors recognized my name and purchased copies by the dozens. B&N flew me out for a special author event.

That dream remains on my pillow, where it is likely to stay. Realistically, I have a better chance of winning the lottery than having my self-published book featured at a brick-and-mortar store. The system of discounts and returns is stacked against me and other self-published authors.

Traditionally published books are distributed as follows:

- The publisher sells the book to a distributor or wholesaler at up to a 70 percent discount from the suggested retail price.
- The distributor or wholesaler then sells the book to a retailer at a 40 to 55 percent discount from the suggested retail price.
- The retailer then sells the book to readers at whatever price it chooses.
- If the books don't sell, the retailer sends the books back through the chain and gets a refund.

Suppose the publisher sets the suggested retail price of a book at $15.00. The distributor or wholesaler buys it from the publisher for $4.50, then turns around and sells it to the retailer for $7.50. The retailer puts the book on its shelves at $12.99. If the book doesn't sell, the retailer returns the book to the wholesaler, who then returns it to the publisher, and everyone gets all or most of their money back. The publisher is stuck with boxes of unsold books and sells them cheap to a remainder company.

Now, place the self-published author in the scenario. Your suggested retail price is $15.00. Your local bookstore, let's say Copperfield's here in Sonoma County, orders three copies through a wholesaler at a 50-percent discount ($7.50 per copy). To make a profit, the wholesaler buys your book from the POD provider at a 70-percent discount ($4.50 per copy). Assuming the POD provider charges you $3.50 per copy plus shipping, you will make a few nickels on each copy sold. And if the books are returned by the retailer, all you get is a loss.

DISCOUNT RATE: DOES IT MAKE ANY DIFFERENCE?

Before you launch your book, you will need to select a discount rate at which your book will be sold to wholesalers. Many SPSCs and POD companies permit authors to set their own discount rate at something between 20 and 70 percent. Some encourage you to set a high discount, so bookstores will order copies; others do the opposite and urge a low discount rate to increase your earnings.

You must also decide whether you will accept returns of unsold books. Some SPSCs accept returns for you, but they charge a high price for the service whether or not your books are ever distributed to bookstores, and whether or not you ever have any returns. Generally, POD providers do not accept returns.

All this is great in theory, but the truth is that no matter how much you discount your book, you are unlikely to get any shelf space at a brick-and-mortar store. Period.

Retailers are unlikely to sacrifice valuable space to an unknown author. The big publishers have sales teams to promote their books and offer incentives ($$) to have their books featured in windows and on table displays. Plus, they offer a range of titles you'll never match. For most self-published authors, hiring a sales team is not in the budget.

When SPSCs and POD providers purport to provide "distribution to major retailers," it means your book will be listed in the catalogues of Ingram, Baker & Taylor, and other wholesalers. That's it.

Distribution does not mean your book will appear in stores; only that the stores may order it from catalogues.

The self-publishing experts recommend you set your discount rate as low as possible and focus your efforts on selling your print books through Internet channels such as Amazon, B&N's online store, and other online sellers. Your book will still be available to brick-and-mortar stores, but expect any sales to be special orders by customers.

If you are using offset printing, high discounts are less of a problem because your costs could be cut in half. You could store and ship the books yourself or engage a fulfillment company to store and ship for you. If you are publishing a fine-art book or are expecting to sell a relatively high volume of books, offset is a viable option. But none of this solves the problem of convincing bookstores to buy your book, other than on consignment.

CONSIGNMENT AGREEMENTS

Many independent bookstores will host readings and carry books published by local authors. Instead of buying the books from Ingram or other suppliers, local bookstores get the books directly from you *on consignment*, which means you continue to own the books. The store does not buy them from you, but agrees to try to sell them for you. If they sell the book, they keep a percentage (typically 40 to 50 percent), and the rest goes to you. (They handle sales tax.)

No need to confine yourself to the local bookstore. Contact stores where you grew up, where you vacation, and where you have set your story. My novel, *Coyote Winds*, which is set in eastern Colorado, sells on consignment at Tattered Cover bookstores in Denver.

Don't be surprised and don't object if the store disclaims any responsibility for theft, damage, or lost books. Also, many stores charge a *marketing* or *setup* fee ranging from $25 to $75. While this is an unfair burden on the self-published author, most independent bookstores operate on thin profit margins. If you cannot afford the fee, ask the store if they will waive it.

Consignment agreements usually expire after 90 days, but in my experience, the stores keep the books on their shelves for a lot longer.

MARKETING OPTIONS FOR E-BOOKS BEYOND KINDLE

The majority of e-books are sold in Kindle format through Kindle Direct Publishing (KDP), a part of Amazon, But don't ignore other distributors and formats such as Apple's iBooks and Kobo. You have two basic options for placing your book in these channels:

- Go to each retailer's site, open an account, convert your manuscript into their digital format, and upload your work, or

- Upload your manuscript to an "aggregator" such as SmashWords, and let them handle conversion and distribution to the other channels.

According to its website, SmashWords has helped over 170,000 authors distribute over 200,000 e-book titles. The company puts your manuscript through its "meat grinder" to convert it into the various e-book formats and distributes the formatted e-book files to the various retail channels. You select the channels, set the pricing, and determine how much of your work is available for a free sample download. They pay you 85 percent of the net-sales proceeds for sales through SmashWords and 60 percent of the list price for sales through other retailers. You may "unpublish" at any time, so it is easy to suspend distribution through SmashWords while you are participating in KDP

Select. Wait at least two weeks after you unpublish before signing up for KDP Select, since it may take that long, if not longer, for your e-book to disappear from other sites. If KDP Select finds your e-book available from other retailers (and it will), they will cancel your KDP Select election and your promotions.

However, if your book contains photographs, charts, graphs, bullet points, or other complex formatting, then you are better off hiring someone to convert the manuscript into the various e-book formats. The meat grinder technique is not reliable. You could end up with a choppy mess on your hands.

No matter how you convert your manuscript, check the final result in each format. It is a tedious task, but far better than distributing garbled content.

KINDLE DIRECT PUBLISHING SELECT

KDP Select is an optional program offered through Amazon. If you sign up for the program, you agree to sell your e-book *exclusively* through Amazon for a period of 90 days and to suspend sales through all other digital channels, including SmashWords, iBookstore, and your own website. This does not affect print and audio books; you may continue to distribute them through any channels. In return, the e-book is available for lending to Amazon Prime members and through the Kindle Unlimited Program, and you will receive a share of revenues from those programs.

In addition

- the e-book earns higher royalties in some countries, and
- you may choose between two promotional tools: Kindle Countdown Deals (limited-time promotional discounting) or Free Book Promotions (free downloads for up to five days in every 90-day period).

Kindle Countdown Deals and Free Book Promotions are so popular there are thousands of discounted and free e-books offered every day. Online, you'll find plenty of advice on how to manage and promote your Kindle promotional days. They get the books into the hands of more readers. Since nothing sells books better than word-of-mouth, these readers will hopefully become more mouths to spread the word.

AVOIDING SCAMS AND MYTHS

Wherever money is to be made, scammers are scheming to take it from you. They promise income, exposure, and freedom from your day job. They brag about off-the-chart successes. If your books are not selling well, you will be tempted to listen to them. Authors are particularly vulnerable since anyone who writes a book tends to be a dreamer. We hope to find the secret formula to success. Perhaps for $99, we will be admitted into that exclusive club.

In all fairness, not all of these offers are scams; some of these companies are selling *myths*. They deliver the listing, the blog tour, the tweets, or other service they promise, but the boost in sales never happens. Myths are a waste of money, just like scams.

If you are under 25 or over 65, you are the prime target for scammers and aggressive salespeople. Younger writers may not have the experience to recognize a con or a pressured sale, and older writers tend not to ask questions for fear of appearing out-of-touch, out-of-date, or simply slow or cranky. Scammers and aggressive salespeople know this and take advantage of it. They prey on your wish to be someone special and to be remembered. Be careful.

When someone is asking you to part with your money, don't let them intimidate, entice, or guilt you into buying a service you do not need or into paying above-market prices. You have the right to ask as many questions as you want. You have the right to say no. You have the right to hang up on them. Go ahead. You'll enjoy the feeling of control.

Some common offers for separating you from your cash:

Companies that charge for services that are virtually free. For example, U.S. copyright registration costs $35 plus two copies of your book and takes about ten minutes. I cannot see paying someone $150 or $200 for the service. For the same reason, I would not pay good money to someone to upload my manuscript to CreateSpace or KDP, which is free; or to set up a Twitter, Pinterest, or other social media site for me, something I could also do myself for free. I have no problem with a company charging clients for these services to help them save time, as long as the clients understand they could have uploaded their manuscripts or set up their social media accounts themselves.

Algorithm-busters. Before long, you will receive offers for software and services to enhance your searchability on Amazon, Google, and other sites. There are companies that claim to have cracked Google's and Amazon's algorithms, but much of their advice is speculation and is available for free on various blogs. There's no need to cough up $49 or $99 or $199 for this service.

Book fairs. Some companies offer you a chance to appear and sign books at their tables at prestigious book fairs. The price? A mere $1,000 and up. You might be "invited" from a select group. Before you jump at the opportunity, look into the book fair. If you team up with a few other authors, you might be able to get your own table at the fair at a fraction of the price.

Literary agents or publishers who charge reading fees. Any legitimate literary agent or publisher will *not* charge a reading fee.

Avoid any agent or publisher who charges to read, review, pre-screen, or evaluate your work.

SPSCs and vanity presses that mislead. Some SPSCs are, or border on being, scams. I am not talking about charging exorbitant fees, which is bad enough. If the company is up-front about its fees and writers sign on anyway, then the writers have some responsibility for their own gullibility or laziness. However, if an SPSC promises services that it does not deliver, performs substandard work (including delays), charges hidden fees, claims exclusive or perpetual rights to the author's work, or fails to report and pay royalties honestly, then that SPSC is a *scammer*, if not worse. I include in that category any SPSC or vanity publisher that pretends to be selective about the projects it accepts, as if it were a traditional press. Such companies convince unsuspecting writers that they have achieved an honor, and the prize is to part with their hard-earned money and sometimes their copyright.

So-called religious presses. Most religious SPSCs and presses are legitimate. But I have seen websites for companies that call themselves Christian. The sites are laced with comfort words like *values, trust*, and *community*, yet have the most egregious and over-reaching contracts, including appropriating people's copyrights. This is the lowest form of scam—hiding behind a religious façade. Don't be fooled.

Getting on *the* list. There's nothing hotter than being on the right list. I'm not talking about bestseller lists here, but lists that claim to give you a competitive edge in the industry. For example, for $50 or $250 or $3,500, some companies promise to get you on the list of hot book-group recommendations, popular school visitors, compelling public speakers, or new and noteworthy releases. Some of these lists are miles long. So much for selectivity.

Radio and media packages. Do not be surprised to get a call or email from a purported radio program or media company eager to interview you. They promise to feature your interview in hundreds of media outlets, because they LOVE your work. There's a catch. To get any more than the basic Internet interview, you will need to cough up a media promotion fee of up to $5,000.

Bogus industry review sites: Some sites pretend to be legitimate, unbiased sites that assist you in choosing the right SPSC for your book. But look at the site carefully, especially the fine print at the bottom. The site could be operated by an SPSC. For instance, chooseyourpublisher.com, e-bookspublishing.com, and poetry-publishers.com are all owned by Author Solutions, a large SPSC which has been sued for misleading marketing practices and breach of contract.

Contests: the real and the unreal. There are many prestigious and legitimate contests. Some are genre specific, such as the Bram Stoker Award for horror, the Prometheus Award for science fiction, and the Scott O'Dell Award for children's historical fiction. Some are open to self-published works; others are not. Some are vague. If they don't prohibit indie books, jump in and give them a try.

However, most contests require an entry fee, and whenever there is money involved, there are sharks. Contests are big money makers. With entry fees ranging as high as $150, a contest with 2,000 entrants earns $300,000.

Your inbox will be flooded with invitations to enter contests. The sponsors run full-color ads in writers' magazines. They also advertise on Craigslist.

Here are some questions to help you sort the good from the bad and the ugly:

Who is the sponsor? Is the sponsor a live person or a publication? If the sponsor is a "media" company, such as J. M. Northern Media (which seems to do nothing but sponsor writing contests with sizeable entry fees), you will gain no prestige by winning. Search the contest on Goodreads, Library Thing, or other writers' communities online. If there's no mention of the contest winners, that's a good indication that the contest lacks prestige. Check out the contest's reputation on writing forums such as Absolute Write Water Cooler, Predators and Editors, and Writers Beware.

How high are the fees? Anything over $30 is suspect. If the sponsor is a reputable literary journal or a legitimate writer's conference, a higher fee is acceptable. Those organizations are often starved for cash.

Who are the judges? You would be surprised how many contests do not disclose the names of the judges. They use vague terms like "industry experts." Some contests are "judged" by reader voting, a recipe for cheating.

How many categories are there? The more categories, the more likely the contest is merely a money maker.

Do they offer you anything for your money? Some contests offer written critiques or reviews for anyone who places, which may make the entry fee worthwhile.

What are the prizes? A roll of stickers? A certificate printed on someone's inkjet? An invitation to attend a book "festival" at your own expense? Can you find online photos of this supposed festival?

What rights are you giving away? Read the fine print, particularly regarding what commitments you are making. I have seen online contests that ask you to post the first 5,000 words of your book. The small print says you are granting the contest sponsor the right to use those words any way it pleases, even in advertising, without your consent or knowledge.

Are they offering a book contract? If the contest offers publication as a prize and you win, are you granting the sponsor first publishing rights? If so, who will be the publisher? Is it a legitimate press with a catalogue of books? Or is it a self-publishing service company or a vanity press? Are you committed to use that publisher if you win, or can you take a cash prize instead? You would hate to have committed your book to one of these contest sponsors if a traditional publisher comes knocking at your door.

For instance, look at the fine print for Amazon's behemoth Breakthrough Novel Award for 2013:

*By submitting an Entry and if you are selected as a Quarter-Finalist or Semi-Finalist, you grant Amazon Publishing **the exclusive first publication rights to your Entry in all formats...***

Translation: If you are a quarter- or semi-finalist, you cannot sell the book to another publisher or publish it yourself if Amazon publishes it. The agreement goes on to say...

If you are not a Winner and Amazon Publishing notifies you that it wishes to publish your Entry, you agree to negotiate the terms and conditions of a publishing agreement exclusively with Amazon Publishing for a period of 30 days after you receive notification from Amazon Publishing. If you and Amazon Publishing have not reached agreement after 30 days, you may offer the work to other publishers on the condition that before you enter into an agreement with another publisher, you will afford Amazon Publishing the last right to publish your Entry on the same terms and conditions offered by any other publisher, plus an advance against royalties 10% greater than the other offer.

Translation: Even if you don't win, they get a second bite at your apple. If your work is burdened by Amazon's right to match other offers, traditional publishers may lose interest.

Finally, everyone who enters the Amazon contest agrees to stop shopping their manuscripts to agents during the six-month contest period. Six months!

The 2013 Amazon contest had 10,000 entries (the cap imposed by Amazon). The Grand Prize winner and First Prize winner each received cash advances and a publishing contract— with an Amazon-affiliated publisher. This may be the breakthrough opportunity of a lifetime. But winning this contest also excludes the sale of your manuscript to any other publisher. As of this writing, many independent bookstores refuse to carry books printed by an Amazon imprint, so the winners of the Amazon Breakthrough Award are unlikely to see their books at brick-and-mortar stores. Seems like a lot to give up for a one in 10,000 possibility of winning.

GENERAL GUIDELINES ABOUT SCAMS AND MYTHS

Don't let ego affect judgment. Flattery softens resolve. If a vendor is overly flattering, give your wallet to someone for safekeeping, particularly someone cynical.

If anything seems too good to be true, it is too good to be true.

Be skeptical of companies that justify higher prices by promising more than their competitors. If they are that good, they would be too busy for your business.

Beware of braggarts. They could turn out to be all talk and no action.

Read testimonials. Are they from the same three people? One person (the owner)? Search those names. Do these people exist? Have they sold a lot of books?

Does the company have a physical address and phone number?

Are you being pressured to decide immediately? If the sales pitch is a one-time offer good for today only, call their bluff. Or better yet, walk way. This sales technique is called "hot boxing" and is an unfair business practice.

See what comes up when you do an online search of the company name plus words like scam, or complaints, or sucks. What you find may be eye opening.

Find out how long the company has been in business. Did they used to operate under another name? Search that name and the name of any people involved with the company. If you see a long string of company names, that is a bad sign.

Search websites such as Predators and Editors, Absolute Write Water Cooler, and Writers Beware. They perform a tremendous service by outing disreputable companies and warning writers.

Develop a good sense of humor. Laugh off these scams. You know better.

MARKETING AND DISTRIBUTION CHECKLIST

In this chapter, we have explored methods for promoting your book, including

- ✓ creating a marketing plan that identifies and focuses on your audience,
- ✓ obtaining reviews,
- ✓ selecting advertising channels,
- ✓ sending out e-blasts without crashing your website,
- ✓ being realistic about your book appearing on bookstore shelves,
- ✓ setting discount rates,

- ✓ entering into consignment agreements with bookstores,
- ✓ expanding beyond Kindle for e-book distribution, and
- ✓ avoiding scams and myths.

We have only just begun. A key component of marketing is building your online presence, also known as your *platform*. If you will be blogging, tweeting, and distributing content, you need a basic understanding of the legal regulations governing the distribution of content on the Internet. Stay tuned: that's up next.

CHAPTER SIX

DMCA, SPAM, AND COPPA

Navigating the Alphabet Soup of the Internet

In addition to wearing the hats of a writer and publisher, you must don the caps of blogger, tweeter, Pinterester, and platform builder. Your Internet duties will feel endless. How many followers and likes are enough? Are your Google Analytics robust? Does anyone click on a privacy policy? You will miss the days when all a writer needed to worry about was her characters' dilemmas.

Maintaining an Internet presence through a website, blog, and on various social media sites raises a number of legal risks and responsibilities. I have already covered the risks of using images and content without permission, and Chapter Seven addresses defamation and invasion of privacy issues. Let's look at some of the legal and regulatory responsibilities triggered by a Web presence.

THE TEN DOS AND DON'TS OF BLOGGING

1. **Don't borrow or steal.** Images, music, and other content you find on the Internet may belong to someone else. Get permissions.

2. **Don't go negative.** Before you launch into a potentially defamatory rant, take a look at Chapter 7. Don't give your target a good reason to sue you.

3. **Don't SPAM.** Nobody likes it, and it violates the law.

4. **Don't divulge.** Privacy is not to be treated lightly. Once a secret is released into the blogosphere, it can never be retrieved.

5. **Don't solicit investors.** Contributions are acceptable, but offering investments to the general public violates securities law.

6. **Do monitor comments.** You may be responsible for defamatory comments, so delete them.

7. **Do adopt a privacy policy.** Check online for samples.

8. **Do disclose compensation and affiliations, no matter how small.** If you are reviewing a book you received for free, say so.

9. **Do verify information.** So much information on the Internet is flat-out wrong. If you repeat a defamatory statement, you could be as liable as the person who made it up. Before you repeat information, confirm it with a reliable source (not Wikipedia). What would a fact-checker do?

10. **Do give credit.** Give credit to those who provide ideas, information, and support. Blogging, after all, is about community. Be a positive part of it.

DMCA AND TAKEDOWN NOTICES

The Digital Millennium Copyright Act (DMCA) provides a mechanism for quick removal of infringing material from the Internet by the delivery of takedown notices.

I have sent takedown notices. A few months ago, I found a link on a YouTube video that read *for a free copy of Coyote Winds, click here.* I clicked and was taken to a Russian website that asked me to register with my name, address, birthday. I stopped. It was a scam, and I did not want *my novel* associated with a scam. I went to the bottom of the YouTube page and clicked on COPYRIGHT. I filled in a simple online form. Now the link reads *This video is no longer available due to a copyright claim by Helen Sedwick.*

If you find your work posted on YouTube, Facebook, Tumblr, Pinterest, or anywhere else online, and you are reasonably confident the posting is *without permission* and is not *fair use*, then you have the right, under the DMCA, to send a takedown notice to the online service and have the infringing work removed. Most social media sites provide an easy online process for submitting a takedown notice.

If your work is posted on a website other than social media, the process is more complicated. Start with emailing the website owner and requesting removal. If that does not work, send the takedown notice to the Internet service provider (ISP) hosting the website. To identify the ISP, try searching the domain name on WhoIs and DomainTools.

The takedown notice must

- be in writing,
- be signed by you, as the copyright owner, or your agent (an electronic signature is sufficient),

- identify the copyrighted work,
- identify the material infringing your work,
- include your contact information,
- state you are complaining in "good faith," and
- state "under penalty of perjury, that the information contained in the notification is accurate."

Sample takedown notices are available online. The National Press Photographers Association (NPPA) site and IPWatchdog have good samples. There are sites that will search the web and send takedown notices for you, for a fee.

In 99 percent of the cases, the social media site or ISP takes down the infringing material, and the matter stops there. But then there's the one percent that don't comply. The user of your content may dispute the takedown claim.

First, you may have given the user permission to use your work without realizing it. For instance, if you posted the material on a critique site such as WEbook or Critique Circle, you may have given them permission to use your material in advertising and promoting their site.

The same is true with Facebook and Google+. Look at the *terms of use* of the site. You may be able to delete your material from their site and terminate their right to use it. Maybe not. The terms of use could say they have a perpetual worldwide license. The devil is in the details.

Second, the use may be fair use. The law permits others to use copyrighted work for commentary, news reporting, reviews, educational purposes, and similar uses. Even if you do not like what they say, they have a right to say it.

Third, the user may lie. They may claim they have the right to use your copyrighted work. If the user disputes your takedown notice, the infringing material will probably reappear, and you are stuck. To stop the unauthorized use, you may have to hire a lawyer and sue. However, hiring an attorney won't be worth it for most self-publishers. Damages (lost sales) may be small and difficult to prove. The infringer may be overseas and unreachable. Also, litigation consumes money like wildfire, not to mention time, attention, and sleep.

DMCA ABUSE

Suppose you post material warning other writers about the egregious business practices of an SPSC, and you quote promises from their website, which you believe are misleading. And suppose the SPSC sends your ISP a takedown notice claiming that your use of those quotes and their name infringes upon their copyright and trademark rights. Most likely, your post will be removed by the social media site or your ISP, even though the DMCA claim is bogus. This is DMCA abuse.

If your material is taken down because of a bogus DMCA notice, dispute it. The process is as simple as filing a DMCA takedown claim in the first place. If your dispute appears legitimate, there is a good chance the social media site or ISP will repost the material.

DMCA abuse is common. Product makers use takedown notices to make unfavorable reviews disappear. Parodies, which are protected as fair use, have been taken down by oil companies. The Electronic Frontier Foundation (EFF) helps writers and other artists fight these abuses. They maintain the Takedown Hall of Shame at https://www.eff.org/takedowns, which is worth a look.

The abuse of DMCA takedown notices is a classic example of the law of unintended consequences. When Congress passed the DMCA in 1998, its goal was to promote free speech by protecting copyright owners as well as the websites that post content created by others. They did not expect DMCA to be used to chill free speech.

CAN-SPAM

The CAN-SPAM Act covers any electronic message with the primary purpose of commercial advertising or promotion, including emails you send to friends about an upcoming reading. While no one is likely to care about your email, if you plan to send out email blasts and/or newsletters to promote your book, follow these common-sense guidelines:

- Don't change the FROM line or your domain address in your header. Phishers use this technique to send out emails purporting to be from banks, PayPal, and eBay. I am clueless about how it is done, but I have seen SPAM messages sent out under my name and my law firm's domain name that were not sent by me.

- Don't use deceptive subject lines. We have all received emails with subject lines saying we've won the lottery, only to find the message is pure advertisement. Don't be cute and try to trick people.

- Identify your message as an advertisement. A simple way is to add a tag line after your signature.

- Allow recipients to opt out of future emails and honor their opt-out requests. Again, a tag line with a link to a designated email will work.

- If you hire a publicist or other person to send out promotional and advertising emails on your behalf, monitor their compliance with SPAM laws. You could be held responsible for their mistakes.

There are penalties for noncompliance, but I hope the FTC is too busy chasing down the phishers and scammers to care about struggling writers trying to sell a few books. But then again, we are easier targets.

PRIVACY POLICIES

You have seen them thousands of times: links to the privacy policy at the bottom of a website page. Should you have one?

You do not need a privacy policy if your website or blog just sits there. If your website and blog consist solely of reading material, and you collect no personal information about your viewers, then you are not required to have a privacy policy.

However, if you collect *personal and identifiable information* to send newsletters, or if you require readers to register and log-in in order to comment on your site or enter a giveaway, or if you post photos of and reviews by your readers, then draft and conspicuously post a privacy policy on your website and blog. In California, it is now the law.

What is personal and identifiable information? Names, addresses, email addresses, phone numbers, user names, passwords, marital status, credit and financial information, medical history, travel itineraries, photographs, Social Security Numbers, or any information in "personally identifiable form."

What about web stats and analytics? Information about your viewers in general, such as browser type, pages viewed, referring sites, history, and location— the sort of information collected by Goggle Analytics—is not considered personal and identifying. I suppose a very sophisticated geek could identify individuals from such data. For this reason, many suggest every website and blog have a privacy policy that at least covers web stats.

What goes into a privacy policy?

- Describe the kind of information collected, such as names, addresses, and credit-card numbers. Provide the user a way to correct errors.

- Explain how the information will be used and shared. Do you share it with potential publishers, agents, publicists, or marketing companies? How do you maintain security?

- Include an opt-out option.

- If you will be collecting personal information about children under the age of 13, then you must comply with the Children's Online Privacy Protection Act (COPPA).

- If you are not aiming your site to children under 13, state something along these lines in your privacy policy: *This site is directed to adults and not directed to children under the age of 13. I ask that minors not submit any personal information. This site complies with the Children's Online Privacy Protection Act and does not permit registration by, and will not knowingly collect personally identifiable information from, anyone under 13.*

COPPA

If you operate a commercial website, online service, or app directed toward children under 13 and collect personal information from those children, then you must comply with a long list of requirements under the Children's Online Privacy Protection Act (COPPA). COPPA also applies if you operate a general-audience website and have actual knowledge that you are collecting, using, or disclosing personal information from children under 13.

For example, if you operate a website where children may share questions and discussions about your book; or upload photos and drawings using their real or user names, home towns, etc., then you must comply with COPPA.

COPPA basics:

- Post a clear and comprehensive online-privacy policy.
- Obtain verifiable parental consent.
- Give parents the choice of prohibiting disclosure to third parties.
- Provide parents a way to review, correct, and delete information.
- Take reasonable steps to maintain confidentiality and security.
- Retain personal identifiable information only as long as necessary.

After reading this list, I have more questions than answers. How am I supposed to obtain verifiable parental consent? What if the child lies about her age? What are reasonable steps to maintain confidentiality? If I have ads on my site, and the children click through to other sites, am I responsible for the practices of these other sites? What is a clear and comprehensive privacy policy?

The COPPA rules are technical, constantly changing, and beyond the scope of this book. If your site is subject to COPPA, educate yourself starting with the FTC website.

I suggest you hire an expert to help set up your site, write your privacy policy, and install parental verification systems. Search online for COPPA *compliance experts*, and you'll find dozens of companies.

As always, research the reputation of these companies before you agree to any contract.

GIVEAWAYS

Have you ever glanced at the back of a Publishers Clearing House sweepstakes mailing? There are about 2,000 words in four-point type about liability, probability, and eligibility. Did you know that the laws that require that microprint apply to your book giveaways as well?

Giveaways and contests are subject to an array of technical laws on the federal and state level, something writers seem to forget in their ongoing battle against obscurity. Few know that asking someone to "like" you on Facebook, "follow" you on Twitter, or subscribe to or comment on your blog as a condition to entering a giveaway could subject them to substantial fines.

As far as I know, federal and state regulators have not cracked down on author giveaways. In case the situation changes, here are a few basics.

There are three types of promotions:

- A *sweepstakes* offers a prize based upon random selection. You *may not* charge a fee or ask for any "consideration of value."

- A *contest* involves some test of skill, and you may charge a reasonable fee.

- A *lottery* awards a prize by random selection and charges a fee. Do not run anything that looks like a lottery. That's illegal.

Most book giveaways, such as those on Goodreads, are sweepstakes because the winners are chosen at random and without charge. They generate buzz and get your books into readers' hands. I have run two successful giveaways on Goodreads myself.

If you want to run a giveaway on your blog or on a social media site, take the time to do it correctly. As I have mentioned earlier, the relationship between a writer and readers depends on trust. Lose their trust and you'll lose your readers.

Don't require consideration. Don't go too far in asking participants to like, retweet, post, subscribe, or sign up as a condition to entering the giveaway. Requiring too much effort could be deemed *consideration* and transform your giveaway from a sweepstakes to an illegal lottery. Using an app such as Rafflecopter won't protect you. According to their terms of service, Rafflecopter leaves it up to you, the *Admin*, to ensure compliance with laws.

Never ask for money for a giveaway. On Kickstarter or other crowdfunding sites, do not offer to give a copy of your book to a contributor chosen at random. That's an illegal lottery. It's better to offer a copy of your book to anyone contributing over a stated amount, such as $75.

Contests are different. If you are running a contest *where skills are judged*, then you may charge a reasonable amount to cover costs and prizes. Do not introduce any element of chance into your contest, such as "if there's a tie, the winner will be chosen by the toss of a coin." That converts your contest into an illegal lottery.

Post rules and procedures in easy-to-read language. Whether you are running a giveaway or a contest, post the following, at a minimum:

- *Who may enter.* To avoid violating the laws of certain countries and states, limit your promotion to entrants in the United States who are at least 18 years old. If your contest is aimed toward children, comply with COPPA.

- *How to enter.* Keep it simple.

- *Timing.* When the giveaway or contest will begin and end.

- *Selection process.* The method or the criteria by which winners will be selected.

- *Odds of winning.* Include language such as "the odds of winning depends on the number of entries."

- *What happens to unclaimed prizes.* Donating them to your local library will work.

- *Discretionary action.* If your entrants are submitting content (stories, photos, etc.), say you have the discretion to eliminate any content you find defamatory, obscene, inappropriate, or potentially infringing.

- *State NO PURCHASE NECESSARY. VOID WHERE PROHIBITED.* These words won't take all the fun out of the promotion. Readers skim over them.

- *Update your privacy policy.* Since you will be collecting personal information, make sure your privacy policy includes a candid discussion on how you will use the information.

- *Reporting.* If the value of the prize is $600 or more, you must deliver a 1099 MISC to the winner and the IRS.

- *Registering.* If the sum of your prizes exceeds $5,000, you may have to register in some states.

If you are running your promotion on Facebook, Twitter, or other social media sites, comply with their policies as well, which change frequently. They are sometimes written in techie jargon, which is worse than legal jargon. If you violate their rules, your account may be suspended or terminated.

To me, it makes the most sense to run your giveaway on well-known book-community sites, since they already have the infrastructure set up to conduct a giveaway properly, not to mention millions of members. These sites include

- Goodreads,
- Book Divas (focusing on books for women),
- FreshFiction (focusing on genres fiction), and
- BookLoons (lists contests for adult and young readers).

Each site has policies of its own. Read them before you hit SUBMIT.

ALPHABET SOUP CHECKLIST

Congratulations writer-author-publisher-marketer, and now blogger-tweeter. You have accomplished a great deal, including

- ✓ setting up your website and blog,
- ✓ knowing how and when to send DMCA takedown notices,
- ✓ managing email campaigns in compliance with SPAM rules,
- ✓ posting a privacy policy,
- ✓ adopting a COPPA-compliance program,
- ✓ conducting giveaways without asking too much effort on the part of participants, and
- ✓ generating blog posts and a following.

Let's take a look at what you may say on your blog and what is over-the-line.

CHAPTER SEVEN

PROTECTING YOUR NEST EGG

Avoid Getting Sued

A blogger in Florida is sued by a real-estate developer for alleging financial mismanagement. The mother of a middle schooler is sued for calling the principal a stoner. A North Carolina blogger is sued for questioning a judge wearing a political campaign button.

With the rise of the Internet, the number of cases alleging defamation, false light, and invasion of privacy has ballooned.

The Internet, after all, offers the opportunity for small voices to be heard worldwide. Misconduct is exposed, wrongs are righted, and potential victims are forewarned. But the Internet is also awash with rumors and falsehoods. Vitriolic rants go viral and ruin reputations. At its worse, cyberbullying has triggered suicide.

As a writer, your goal is to uncover truths, both large and small, about yourself and the world. How do you write about people you know without risking a lawsuit? How do you post about injustice or unfairness without losing your home to legal bills?

The laws of defamation and privacy try to balance the interest of the individual against society's interest in promoting free speech and discussion. As with any area where the law tries to balance interests, it is a mess. The statutes vary state by state and country by country. Scholars have written enough commentary to fill a small library, and they still disagree. Case rulings are inconsistent and arbitrary since they reflect the values and attitudes of judges and juries and not the black-letter law.

And because the cases typically involve allegations of criminality, infidelity, promiscuity, paternity, or idiocy, the emotions are explosive.

Common sense and a cool head are key to avoiding trouble. So is a basic understanding of the law. The following information summarizes United States law. The laws of other countries, particularly Great Britain and France, are more favorable to the targets of defamatory statements. Beware. In today's Internet environment, you could get sued in England for a blog written in California.

DEFAMATION

To prove defamation, whether *libel* for written statements or *slander* for spoken ones, a plaintiff must prove all of the following elements:

False Statement of Fact

If a statement is true, then it is not defamatory no matter how offensive or embarrassing. Truth is a complete defense.

Opinions are also protected. If you post a restaurant review stating a meal was so bad you gagged, you will probably be fine. But one restaurant critic was sued for saying a stringy steak tasted like horsemeat. The plaintiff claimed the reference to horsemeat was a statement of fact and not a colorfully stated opinion.

Couching something as an opinion is not bullet-proof. Courts see no difference between "Joe is a pedophile" and "In my opinion, Joe is a pedophile." The question is whether the statement is "reasonably susceptible of a defamatory connotation." Who decides that? The judge or jury.

To write about egregious conduct, or to voice a complaint or sound a warning, remember the writing rule: *show, don't tell.* Stick to verifiable facts and personal emotional responses, and apply your creative skills to hyperbole and voice.

Suppose your publishing company overcharges you, never returns calls, and produces work riddled with typos. Show us the errors, highlight the charges, poke fun at the botched English of a customer service rep halfway around the globe, but avoid labels like crook, fraud, scammer, and idiot. Trust your readers to understand the message.

Identifiable Person or Company

A defamatory statement must contain sufficient information that would lead a reasonable person (other than the target) to be able to identify the target. Typically, the target must be a *living person*, but a defamatory statement about a corporation might trigger a defamation suit by officers, directors, and employees of the corporation who believe they have been harmed by the false statement.

Companies and groups have the right to sue for defamation. Oprah Winfrey was sued in 1998 by Texas ranchers after saying that she had sworn off eating hamburgers because of mad cow disease. (Oprah won the case.) A group of beef processors is suing ABC News, Diane Sawyer, and others for labeling their lean, finely textured beef as "pink slime."

Suppose you want to base a character on a living person. Change enough details so the person is not recognizable. The more villainous the character, the more changes you should make. The same is true if you are using a company as an evil character, such as a polluter.

Publication or Dissemination

If one person (other than the target) reads or hears a defamatory statement, that is sufficient to support a lawsuit. You may write all the nasty letters you please to the target, but if you post your letters on your blog, or show them to one other person (other than your attorney), you are risking a defamation suit.

Reputational Harm

A false statement must be more than offensive, insulting, or inflammatory. The plaintiff must show the statement "tends to bring the subject into public hatred, ridicule, contempt, or negatively affect the business or occupation of the subject."

Certain statements are assumed to cause harm. These include statements attributing someone with dishonesty, criminal conduct, association with disfavored groups such as street gangs, a physical or mental disease or disability, sexual promiscuity or perversion, impotence, or professional incompetence.

Context is important. A target may be harmed more by false statements in the *New York Times* than a parody in *The Onion*, because courts assume readers of *The Onion* understand they are reading humorous content. Much depends on the facts of the case.

Made With Actual Malice

If the target is a public official or a public figure, and the statement relates to the arena in which they are in the public eye, then the plaintiff must prove the statement was made with actual malice. Malice does not mean an intention to harm. It means actual knowledge that the statement was false or was made with a reckless disregard for the truth. The standard is high; the defendant/writer must have had a reasonable basis to know the statements were false. Actual malice may also be shown if the defendant refuses to publish a retraction after being shown the original statements were false.

Negligence

Historically, if you made a false and defamatory statement against a private individual, you would have liability even if you took every reasonable precaution to determine its veracity. In recent years, courts are requiring some measure of fault or negligence on the part of the defendant. For this reason, keep a record of your factual sources in case you ever have to disprove a claim of negligence. Retain interviews and copies of relevant materials.

Make sure you have your names right. If you report true facts about Robert Paulson, but carelessly type it out as Robert Peterson, Mr. Peterson may have a claim against you.

Don't try to hide behind attributing false statements to someone else or using fudge words like "it has been reported that ..." and linking to or identifying a source may not protect you. It depends on whether it was reasonable for you to rely on the source. Do your homework. Fact-check. You could be held liable for repeating a defamatory statement.

ANONYMOUS STATEMENTS

Some people try to avoid liability by posting defamatory statements anonymously. With enough money and technology, they are typically found out.

INDEMNIFICATION CLAUSES

Another reason to be careful: when you clicked ACCEPT on the contract with your SPSC, POD provider, and ISP, chances are you agreed to *indemnify, defend, and hold them harmless* from any claim of infringement, defamation, invasion of privacy, and a whole host of other horribles. Translation: if these companies are named in any lawsuit based upon your writings and publications, you must hire and pay the attorneys to defend them and you must pay their costs and damages if you lose or settle.

THE M.E. FACTOR

As an attorney, I am often asked, "Can someone sue me?" Unfortunately, just about anyone may sue you. Their case may not survive the first round of legal battles, but someone can still initiate and file a lawsuit even if it is frivolous. My rule of thumb about litigation risk is the *M.E. Factor,* money multiplied by emotion. If a lot of money is involved, then a lawsuit is likely even if there is little anger or emotion surrounding the dispute. On the other hand, if someone is angry, offended, or feels threatened, then they are likely to sue regardless of a small financial stake. Don't assume no one will go after you because you have no money. If you get someone peeved enough, you may awake one morning to a process server banging on your door.

You don't want to live your life hiding under a rock. Always reach for the truth when writing—it's the best defense.

INSURANCE

Your homeowner's insurance might provide coverage for defamation claims if they arise from negligence, meaning you took reasonable measures to verify all factual statements. But a homeowner's policy may not cover business pursuits, so ask your insurance agent if you should purchase a business-liability policy or endorsement. None of these policies will cover intentional acts if you knowingly made a false and defamatory statement. Check with your insurance carrier *now* before claims are made.

SLAPP AND ANTI-SLAPP

If you speak out on a matter of significant controversy involving well-financed interests, you may find yourself the target of a *SLAPP*. A SLAPP (Strategic Lawsuit Against Public Participation) is a lawsuit filed with intent to censor, intimidate, and silence critics from exercising their First Amendment rights. The most common form of SLAPP is a defamation claim.

Journalists and bloggers are hit with SLAPPs for exposing truthful information, albeit unpleasant, illegal, or embarrassing. We can assume the plaintiff who filed the suit expects to lose the case, particularly if the information is verifiable, but the goal is to silence the offending speech without stepping into a courtroom. Of course, SLAPP plaintiffs do not admit such motivations. The defendant (perhaps you) must put up a fight. How many writers can afford expensive and drawn-out court battles?

Most states have passed Anti-SLAPP laws that entitle a successful defendant to recover attorneys' fees, but you would have to prevail in court, which could easily take years.

If you are threatened or hit with a lawsuit that seems motivated by spite or intimidation, skip to Chapter Ten and seek legal counsel immediately. Your rights and your wallet are at risk.

IF YOU'RE THE TARGET…

What if someone posts false statements of fact about you that harm your reputation? Immediately ask for a retraction, and if that does not work, consult with an experienced attorney. But before you sue, ask yourself whether suing will only call more attention to a matter best forgotten.

INVASION-OF-PRIVACY CLAIMS

Even if you publish the truth and nothing but the truth, you may still be sued for invasion of privacy. If you disclose embarrassing or unpleasant facts about an *identifiable, private person* that are offensive to ordinary sensibilities and not of overriding public interest, the target may sue you for invasion of privacy, intentional infliction of emotional distress, and other claims.

As a preliminary matter, the target must have a reasonable expectation of privacy to assert a claim. Any conduct or appearance in a public place is not protected, particularly today when almost everyone carries a camera in a pants pocket. Similarly, public figures are often barred from claiming they have any reasonable expectation of privacy. A movie star lounging topless on a yacht a mile from shore should not be surprised that a camera with an extremely long lens is pointing her way.

Another flavor of invasion of privacy is called *false light.* Suppose you post a photo of a criminal arrest. Jane Doe, a bystander, appears in the picture, a true fact. If the photo creates the impression that Jane was arrested and you do not take reasonable measures to dispel that impression, Jane could sue you for portraying her in a false light.

Intrusive fact gathering will also get you into trouble. If you gather private information by hacking, wiretapping, spying, or climbing trees to see into someone's back yard, you could get sued for invasion of privacy and trespass.

Using someone's likeness, name, or identifying information for advertising, promotional, or commercial purposes may get you sued. Whether the person is a private individual or public figure, you would be liable for damages, including punitive damages. If the person is dead, you could still get sued in some states and foreign countries. Obtain a written release before you use anyone's image, name, or identifiable information for commercial or promotional purposes.

BASING CHARACTERS ON FRIENDS AND FAMILY

For most authors, friends and family are the richest sources for fictional characters. The rules outlined above also apply when writing about those close to you. Show, don't tell. Mask distinguishing characteristics.

Pay particular attention to the privacy issues when borrowing events and characters from real life. While your family members may feel flattered (or may miss the similarities altogether), there's a good chance they will feel betrayed and exploited. Family members sue one another all the time. The M.E. factor is particularly high.

If you are writing a "getting even" book (to get back at a parent, spouse, friend, boss, or someone else who made your life miserable), write the manuscript with all the passion of anger, but then put it aside for months, or even years, while you cool down. Only then will you be able to edit it with an analytical eye and make the story more universal, including masking your characters so they are not recognizable.

Or better yet, you could wait until your target has passed away.

MEMOIR, BIOGRAPHIES, HISTORIES

Memoirs, biographies, histories, political commentary, and other non-fiction works require the use of real names and real people, so take particular care to follow the *show, not tell* guidelines and avoid labels. With respect to factual matters, retain records to support your statements. If you are speculating about an event or motivation, be clear you are taking a guess. State your opinions and observations from your point-of-view, not as established facts.

Regarding private matters, ask for consent and/or rely on publicly disclosed information, such as court documents and news reports. (Court filings are a rich source of juicy information.) Inevitably, someone will feel offended, hurt, or perhaps vindicated, even if they do not have a reason to sue. Comes with the territory.

FACTION AND DOCUDRAMAS

If you are creating a work that mixes true facts about living persons with fictional elements such as dialogue and scenes, consult with an attorney. The risks are too complex to be covered here.

OTHER RESTRICTIONS ON USING INFORMATION

Before you use private information, consider whether you are subject to other restrictions. For instance, as an attorney, I cannot use any confidential information about a client, even if I change the name and mask the identity. The same would be true for therapists, doctors, accountants, and other professionals. If you are a trustee, partner, or have a fiduciary relationship with a third party, you have a duty not to bring harm onto the other party by disclosing personal information. So don't do it.

Have you signed a confidentiality agreement? Many public figures require their gardeners, nannies, drivers, maids, chefs, and other staff to sign stringent confidentiality agreements for obvious reasons.

If you were a party to a lawsuit settled out of court, take a look at your settlement agreement. Most likely, it contains nondisclosure and non-disparagement clauses. You could unwind the hard-fought settlement by blabbing.

Will you be disclosing trade secrets or other proprietary information? At your job, you may learn valuable trade secrets such as formulas, marketing plans, and manufacturing details. If you disclose that information, even if it is true, you could find yourself without a job and facing a lawsuit, if not criminal charges, for stealing trade secrets. However, if you are exposing something illegal or dangerous and the action is a SLAPP, get an experienced Anti-SLAPP attorney to assist you.

Don't make threats of physical violence against individuals, the government, or (especially) the President. You could be arrested, and you would find yourself on the NSA's and the FBI's radar.

Obscenity may also pose problems, depending on the local community standards.

As always, when in doubt or when threatened with a lawsuit, seek the advice of experienced counsel.

SAVING YOUR NEST EGG CHECKLIST

✓ Don't say someone is criminal, sexually deviant, diseased, or professionally incompetent or use labels such as *crook, cheat, pervert,* or *corrupt.*

- ✓ Never say something like *"don't do business with xyz company."*
- ✓ Show, don't tell. Stick to verifiable facts and your personal observations, opinions, experiences, and reactions. Let your readers come to their own conclusions.
- ✓ Respect privacy. In today's crowded world, privacy is more valuable than ever.
- ✓ Be mindful of the M.E. Factor. Money multiplied by emotion. Don't discount the power of angry people.
- ✓ If you are the one who's mad as heck, write out your rant, but don't publish it. Send it to someone with a cool head. (It's best if you remove the name of your actual target.) Wait a few days and listen to that person's advice.
- ✓ If you base a character on a real, living person, mask identifying features.
- ✓ Don't use anyone's name or image for commercial purposes without express permission.
- ✓ Add the standard disclaimer to fiction pieces. "This book is a work of fiction. Any resemblance to actual events or persons, living or dead, is entirely coincidental."
- ✓ If accused of a defamatory statement, consider publishing a retraction.

As you have probably noticed by now, I recommend avoiding lawsuits, even if you have done nothing wrong. Litigation and arbitration are more risky and unpredictable than you realize. The process is expensive and incredibly stressful. You are better off spending your time and energy promoting your book and writing the next one.

CHAPTER EIGHT

TAXES

A Few Surprises, Both Good and Bad

The sad fact is over 40 percent of every dollar earned goes back to the government in taxes on the federal, state, or local level. Income taxes, employment taxes, and sales taxes take big bites out of your cash flow, not to mention the hours lost to filling out tax forms. Is there any way to reduce the time and money swallowed up by taxes?

If you followed the steps in Chapter One for obtaining an EIN, resale certificate, and business license; using a DBA; and separating your self-publishing finances from your personal finances, then you are well on your way to saving money and managing your taxes efficiently. The payoff comes at tax time.

What follows is a general overview of the tax issues facing a self-published author. The technical details would fill bookshelves, and this chapter alone cannot cover all scenarios. I have touched on areas where the law has been fairly static for a few years, but tax rulings are always evolving.

As I mentioned earlier in the book, if you ask a lawyer for an opinion about a legal matter, her most likely answer will be "it depends." Every taxpayer's situation is unique. Nowhere is that more true than with tax law.

CIRCULAR 230 DISCLAIMER: If and to the extent that this book contains any tax advice, I am required by the Internal Revenue Service's Circular 230 (31 CFR Part 10) to advise you that such tax advice is not a formal legal opinion and is not intended or written to be used by you, and may not be used by you, (i) for the purpose of avoiding tax penalties that might be imposed on you or (ii) for promoting, marketing or recommending to another party any transaction or matter addressed herein.

INCOME TAXES: RECORDKEEPING AND ORGANIZATION

Most taxpayer problems are due to inadequate recordkeeping. In tax audits, more people are nailed for losing receipts than for cheating. If you don't have a file cabinet (real or virtual) dedicated to your self-publishing business, then get one. Maintain good business records for two reasons: to prove your expenses and deductions, and to demonstrate your self-publishing activity is a business that's for profit and not a hobby.

What records to keep:
- receipts for all expenses,
- royalty statements,
- sales slips and receipts for direct sales,
- appointment books and calendars,
- brochures from conferences to show the events were business-related,
- business cards and manuscript critiques collected at conferences,
- thank-you notes from libraries or schools,

- fan emails,

- contest entries and notifications,

- correspondence with freelancers, whether or not hired,

- letters from agents and publishers, including rejections,

- bank and credit card records,

- printouts of PayPal summaries,

- W9s and 1099s, and

- sales tax returns.

Keep all records for seven years. Some people say three, but if you are starting a business, I suggest seven years in case you have to prove your self-publishing business is not a hobby. I discuss *Hobby Rules* below.

A special note about appointment books and calendars. A simple way to organize your records and build supporting documentation for business-related automobile miles is to use your appointment book or desk calendar. Note all trips to the post office, conferences, readings (including those when you are sitting in the audience), and critique-group meetings. On January 1st of each year, write down your odometer reading and calculate how many of those miles were related to your self-publishing business. If you keep your calendar electronically, print it out and keep a copy with your tax records.

WHAT IS INCOME?

Your writing income will include receipts from royalties, whether paid by check or via electronic transfers into your bank account, direct sales (such as at book fairs), and speaking fees. If someone lends you money, the loan amount is not income (unless the lender forgives the debt). If someone reimburses you for an expense, the reimbursement is not income, as long as you do not deduct the same expense from income. That's double dipping.

If your net income (gross revenues less deductions) from self-publishing is $400 or more in any calendar year, you may be required to pay self-employment tax on your self-publishing income. This includes the employer and employee portions of Social Security tax and Medicare tax. If your taxes on your publishing income exceed $1,000 per year, you may be required to pay quarterly estimated taxes. Sadly, most self-publishing authors won't achieve these levels. I hope you are one of the exceptions.

WHAT IS DEDUCTIBLE?

Ordinary and necessary expenses of operating your business are deductible, including:

- office supplies and postage,
- costs of writing and research books,
- magazine subscriptions,
- telephone charges,
- printing costs for business cards, bookmarks, and postcards,
- advertising costs,
- costs for software, such as design, video-editing, manuscript editing, and analytics,
- fees and royalties paid for fonts, images, music, and other content,
- writing-club dues,
- website hosting and online backup costs,
- subscription costs for HootSuite or other web-based services,

- payments to freelancers, such as editors, copyeditors, designers, web designers, and publicists,
- research expenses, including travel,
- cost of books you give away to reviewers or in promotional giveaways,
- contest entry fees,
- copyright registration fees, and
- a portion of your car and home expenses.

Many expenses incurred in the years prior to your first book launch will be deductible as start-up expenses, so save those receipts as well. If your start-up expenses are less than $5,000, you may deduct them in the first year you operate your business. If they are greater than $5,000, you may need to amortize some of these expenses over a longer period.

Once you are selling books, you may deduct most of your expenses in the year in which you pay them. Remember to obtain a W9 from, and to deliver a 1099 and corresponding state form to each individual to whom you pay $600 or more in any calendar year.

Costs of Goods Sold are deducted differently. The expense of buying inventory is not deductible until you sell that inventory. If in one year you buy 500 books from your POD provider and resell 300, you may deduct the cost of the 300 books sold. The cost of the remaining 200 books is not supposed to be deducted until you sell them.

If you work from home, you may be entitled to a home-office deduction. If you use your car for self-publishing activities, you may deduct a portion of your automobile expenses, including lease or loan payments, repairs, gas, and insurance; or you may take a deduction on a per-mile basis. As I mentioned above, use your datebook or calendar to keep track of your work-related miles during the year.

You may use deductions to offset revenues generated by your self-publishing business. *You may also use deductions to offset other income*, which is a nice surprise to many self-publishing authors. You will lose that benefit if the IRS decides your venture is a hobby and not a business.

HOBBY RULES

You may have heard the old rule that a business is considered a hobby unless it shows a profit during three out of five years. If the IRS decides your business is a hobby, then you may *not* deduct book-related expenses from other income. You may offset those expenses from your self-publishing income only.

In practice, the hobby rule is not as strict as the three-out-of-five-year rule. If you demonstrate you have a *serious intent to operate a business at a profit*, the IRS will generally give you some slack. To demonstrate this intent-

- follow the steps in Chapter One about setting up your business, particularly obtaining an EIN, seller's certificate, and business license,
- maintain separate financial records and bank accounts,
- advertise and otherwise actively promote your books,
- join professional organizations and network,
- attend writing-related conferences, and better yet, speak at them, and
- most importantly, for the IRS and your own well-being, keep working on your next writing project.

Software is available to help complete your tax returns. But nothing replaces a skilled accountant or enrolled agent. These professionals often identify savings that more than cover their fees.

SALES TAXES

Sales taxes are a major headache for most authors. Unless you are selling hundreds of books directly to readers via your website, book fairs, readings, or other venues, the hassle will be disproportionate to the money involved.

But as they say, death and taxes . . . you can't avoid them.

I will not tell you, "Don't worry about it. No one will ever know." With computer technology, the chances of getting hit with penalties and interest are increasing. Below are the basics. The details are enough to drive anyone crazy.

How much is the sales tax? It depends on the location of the buyer. In California, the tax rate varies by city and county. You will have to look it up. Sales tax is based on the selling price of the item, not on net profit from the sale. If you sell a book at $12, but you bought it from your POD provider for $5, you pay sales tax on the entire $12, not on your profit of $7. You have to pay sales taxes even if your self-publishing business is operating at a loss.

What sales are subject to sales tax? It depends. If you sell print books in person, such as at a reading or book fair, or over the Internet to buyers *in your own state*, then by law you are required to pay sales taxes on the print books sold, although you may collect it from buyers.

Twenty-five states are now charging sales tax on digital downloads, so sales tax may apply if you are delivering your e-book or other content directly to buyers via downloads.

If you are filling Internet or telephone orders for a customer in another state, you may also be required to pay sales tax to the buyer's state if you have a business presence (sometimes called a *nexus*) in that state.

What is a business presence? This is controversial. Some states have enacted legislation that requires large online sellers to collect sales tax even if the seller has no physical presence in the state. These laws are referred to as *Amazon laws* for obvious reasons. The rules are full of technicalities and always changing. For most self-published writers, you will be considered to have a presence in the state if you have a home there or are selling the book at venues in that state, such as a conference or book fair.

To make matters even more complicated, the federal government is proposing the Marketplace Fairness Act of 2013, which would permit states to require sellers who are not physically located in their states to collect taxes on online and catalog sales made to people in their states. As drafted, sellers who make $1 million or less in annual sales and have no physical presence in the state would be exempt from this requirement. I suspect the $1 million threshold will be reduced because states want to collect as much tax as possible. I doubt most self-publishers will be affected by this new law, but if you are enjoying hundreds of thousands in direct sales, you should be working with a tax accountant who stays on top of these changes.

NOLO Press has a site that purports to summarize the laws regarding Internet sales tax applicable to interstate transactions. Search *NOLO Press 50-State Guide to Internet Sales-Tax Laws*. I have not researched their links to each state's laws, but it is a good place to start. Also check with your state's website. In California, the State Board of Equalization has dozens of publications regarding sales tax, and many are in Spanish, Korean, Farsi, Thai, and other languages. You can call the state agency and ask questions as well.

Warning: The web is littered with misinformation about sales tax. When in doubt, go to the source, such as the sales-tax publications prepared by your state. Here are some rules to keep in mind:

- If you are selling books from your home state to a buyer in your home state, then you pay sales tax based on the location of the sale, or if you are mailing the book, the location of the buyer.

- If you are selling books at a conference or book fair out of state, then you pay sales tax on books you physically hand over in that state. If you go home and ship books out of state, then the interstate rules apply.

- If you sell your book for a flat amount, let's say $15, write SALES TAX INCLUDED on the receipt. It will be up to you to figure out what portion of the $15 is sales tax.

- More states are applying sales taxes to e-books and other downloads. Expect this trend to continue.

- Shipping and handling charges are not subject to sales tax if they do not exceed your actual costs.

- If the bookstore where you do a reading handles the sales to customers, then it is up to the store to collect and pay the sales tax.

- If you are selling through Amazon and online sites other than your own, they will collect and pay the sales tax.

- If you are using PayPal, Square, or a similar service to process your direct sales, add sales tax to the purchase price. You are responsible for reporting and paying the sales tax collected.

- Go to your local office-supply store and buy a receipt book that makes a carbon copy for each sale. Make a receipt out for customers, and make a receipt for yourself when you give away a book. Keep those receipts and records of your online sales.

The flip side is when you buy books from your POD provider, such as CreateSpace, with the intention of reselling them, you do not have to pay sales taxes on your purchase as long as you have a resale or seller's certificate, as I discussed in Chapter One. Supply the POD provider with a copy of your resale certificate. Sometimes they will accept the certificate number only.

Only items you purchase for resale are exempt from sales tax, namely, your book. Office supplies (paper, ink, etc.), computers, bookmarks, and business cards are subject to sales tax because you are using them, not reselling them.

If you buy books without paying sales tax on your purchase, and instead give the books away to reviewers and friends or submit them to contests, then you are required to report those giveaways as if they were sales at the wholesale price and pay sales tax on each book. I suggest you pay the sales tax to CreateSpace or another POD provider when you purchase copies to be given away.

You will report your sales (including sales to yourself on books given away) on sales-tax returns filed quarterly or annually depending on the state. In California, you can fill in the forms online. Once you register for a resale certificate, the state will hound you for these returns.

There are substantial penalties for failing to file returns (even if you have no sales) and failing to account accurately for sales. You are expected to maintain books and records of all taxable transactions for four years after your annual filing.

You might think it would be easier just to pay your POD provider sales tax on orders you buy so you don't have to worry about calculating, collecting, and paying sales tax when you resell the book.

Not so easy. If you pay your POD provider sales tax that's based on a price of $4 a copy, but then you resell your books for $12 a copy, you are supposed to collect sales tax on the $8 markup and pay it to the state. I have no idea how many people actually comply with any of these requirements.

Ready to throw your hands up in the air? I don't blame you. But keeping track of sales taxes is not as bad as it sounds. If you keep decent records, then filing the returns will not be too time consuming.

TAXES CHECKLIST

To simplify and save on taxes-

- ✓ maintain good records of your business activities, income and expenses,
- ✓ separate your business and personal finances,
- ✓ treat your self-publishing venture as a business, not a hobby,
- ✓ contact your state for sales tax publications, and read them,
- ✓ provide your seller's certificate to your POD provider to avoid sales tax on books you intend to resell,
- ✓ pay sales tax to your POD provider on books you intend to give away,
- ✓ maintain records of all books sold and given away, whether or not they are subject to sales tax,
- ✓ submit your sales tax returns and pay the tax when due,
- ✓ keep working on writing projects, and
- ✓ buy that file cabinet. (It's tax deductible.)

CHAPTER NINE

COLLABORATIONS

The Whole Is Greater Than the Sum of Its Parts

When a writing collaboration works well, partners inspire and complement one another. The writing reaches a higher level. The creative process is less lonely and more fun.

But when the collaboration fails, the drama may be as ugly as a Hollywood divorce.

For every successful writing partnership, there are dozens of failed ones, despite the best of intentions. Not everyone is a team player, and not every team is a winner.

The best way improve the odds of a successful collaboration is to take the time to put the collaboration agreement in writing. Most people resist this idea. Like a prenuptial agreement, it kills the romance. Even if you are best friends or soul mates, write out your agreement. Face tough questions while you are full of optimism.

The process of preparing an agreement may be more valuable than the result. The better job you do in flushing out issues at the start, the less likely you will have problems later on.

TOPICS TO DISCUSS AND PUT IN WRITING

- **Describe your joint project in detail.** This is critically important to clarify what rights you share and what rights, projects, income, and liabilities you won't share. Imagine drawing a box around the project and clearly state what creations are in the box and what are not.

- **Goals, including monetary and nonmonetary goals.** If you do not share common goals, then the partnership won't work. If one partner's objective is to make money with a slapdash genre piece, and the other partner dreams of creating a timeless work of literary fiction, then that partnership will blow up. Be honest with yourself and your partner.

- **Level of commitment.** Are you entering into a full-time commitment, or may the partners work on other projects concurrently? What about competitive projects? If one partner contributes more than the other, is that partner compensated with a larger percentage of the royalties?

- **Who covers expenses?** If one partner pays up-front for research, editing, design, and development costs, does that partner recoup expenses before income is shared? If the project never recoups the expenses, does the other partner have a duty to pay her share?

- **Deadlines.** If you set deadlines, are they realistic? Most projects take twice as long as expected, if not more.

- **Responsibilities.** Is one better at plot and the other at character? What about engaging editors and designers? Who will negotiate contracts, handle interviews, and manage social media? Don't take the shortcut of saying responsibilities will be shared equally. It never happens. People gravitate to the tasks they do better and enjoy more.

- **Expectations.** A scenario I see all too often is that one partner feels the other is not doing her fair share. Or both partners feel that way. Typically, the partners have never had a conversation about expectations. Resentment smolders. Discuss expectations. Do not expect the impossible, and do not promise it either.

- **Writing process.** Perhaps one person will write out the story in narrative form, and the other will flesh out scenes and dialogue. Or maybe you'll each draft chapters and trade them for comments. Some writers work well brainstorming together; others prefer a silent room. Discuss how often you will meet.

- **Decision-making.** You will have disagreements; I guarantee it. View them as a sign that something is not working in the manuscript. Listen to each other. Step back, and then step back some more. Let go of your ego, and look at the problem a new way, or better yet, your partner's way. Chances are you will find an acceptable solution. However, if you cannot resolve the disagreement, then decide who gets the final say. If the project was the idea of one partner, that partner typically gets the final say. Or pick a third party trusted by both sides.

- **No door slamming.** Agree that neither of you will walk out of the partnership without giving the other party notice of what's not working and a reasonable time to work it out. Respect each other's requests for cooling off periods.

- **Reward yourselves.** How will you reward yourselves when you reach milestones? When you finish each chapter, will you open a bottle of champagne? When you complete the first draft, will you take yourselves out to dinner?

- **Credits.** Decide whether both names will appear on the work and in what order. If one name has greater marketing value, put that name first. If you cannot agree, use alphabetical order. Will your credit be listed as A *and* B, A *with* B, or A *as told to* B? The words may be small, but there are big distinctions among them. If you say "and," it implies the writing was shared equally. If you say "with," it means the first name contributed more. If you say "as told to," it indicates B essentially did all the writing. Will the work be published under a pen name?

- **Ownership and copyright.** Unless you agree otherwise, all partners own equal interests in the copyright of a jointly created work, and each partner has the power to sell or license the entire work without the other partner's consent (although income must be shared). Put your ownership percentages in writing. State that neither one of you may sell, license, or transfer any interest in the project without the consent of the other partner. When you register the copyright for the project, register it under both names, or the pen name, or all of the above. Personally, I recommend the partner who had the original idea own the majority interest, even if it is a token amount (51%/49% split). That little percent saves resentment later.

- **Income.** How will income be split? If one partner does events, such as readings or conferences, does that partner keep a larger portion of sales at those events? Will income be paid directly into a joint account?

- **Keeping it legal.** Each partner must promise to the other that all work contributed to the project will be original, will not have been sold or licensed to anyone else, will not infringe on anyone's intellectual property rights, will not be defamatory, and will not invade anyone's privacy or other rights. Don't be foolish about this. If your partner introduces material you suspect is problematic, rewrite it or reject it. If you get sued, *both* of you may be responsible.

- **Collaboration, not partnership.** Although I have referred to writing *partners* throughout this chapter, the agreement should state that the parties are *collaborating* for a specified project and are not creating a *general partnership*. In a partnership, each partner may be liable for the bad acts of the other partners. Stating that the relationship is a collaboration might protect the innocent partner if a third party claims the work is infringing or defamatory.

- **Future projects.** If you or your writing partner plan to create subsequent book projects, such as sequels, prequels, or a series, does your agreement state that you may work on them separately or together only? If you don't work together, can either one of you publish a related work provided the other gets a royalty?

- **Death or disability.** What if one of you gets hit by the proverbial bus? Does the other have the right to finish the project with an equitable adjustment in ownership and allocation of income? Does all decision-making authority transfer to the surviving partner, or will the heirs or representatives of the deceased or disabled partner have a say?

- **Termination.** If the partnership terminates, who owns the work? Who has the right to complete the project? If the project is sold, how will income and credit be shared? There are no right answers here. The partners need to talk this out.

- **What ifs.** What if one of you (or both of you) gets divorced and your soon-to-be ex-spouse claims one-half of the work as community property? Same with personal bankruptcy, but this time the creditors want an interest in the work. What if someone releases a book like yours when the project is 95 percent complete? What if a partner flakes out? What if someone steals your work?

- **Disputes.** Insert a mediation clause. In the event of an irreconcilable dispute, the partners will participate in nonbinding mediation with a professional mediator before resorting to legal action.

Alternatives to collaborations. Collaboration may be the wrong structure for the project. Perhaps one is the writer and the other is an expert, in which case the writer owns the project and the expert is paid a set fee. Or flip this structure, and the expert is the owner and the writer is a ghostwriter paid a flat fee.

CHECKLIST FOR A SUCCESSFUL COLLABORATION

- ✓ Put your collaboration agreement in writing.
- ✓ Respect each other, including accepting each other's shortcomings.

✓ Laugh together, especially when everything is going wrong.

✓ Work from an outline. The outline sets you in the same direction.

✓ Learn how to give and receive criticism well. Be constructive. Refrain from being emotional, so your comments aren't taken personally.

✓ Let the little stuff slide. Entering into a partnership involves giving up some control. Your partner may have a different approach to a scene, a character, or a problem, but consider that a good thing. Listen to another perspective. Be open to new ideas. This is why you are working as a team.

✓ Communicate with each other. Years ago, a friend told me the motto of a happy marriage: "I can't read your f*king mind!" The same is true in writing collaborations.

CHAPTER TEN

LAWYERS

They Are on Your Side

Sooner or later, you will need an attorney. Perhaps your publishing business is expanding to the point where you are considering incorporating and bringing in investors. Maybe your collaboration agreement needs a legal touch. Or, the worst has happened and someone is suing you for infringement, defamation, or some other wrongful act.

Many people have an unfavorable view of attorneys, which is not entirely fair. Yes, some attorneys are bullies, but they would have been bullies no matter what their profession. Most lawyers are bookish types who try to look after their clients. If you avoid the bullies, you'll find attorneys are valuable members of your publishing team.

Business attorneys assist you on matters such as setting up your business, obtaining EINs and resale certificates, drafting licenses and agreements, reviewing manuscripts for potential legal issues, and providing preventive counseling. Choose a business attorney for business/contract issues, intellectual property issues, and regulatory matters, perhaps calling in a specialist for targeted questions. They rarely step into the courtroom. Like me, their goal is to keep their clients out of court. However, if litigation claims arise, a business attorney typically assists clients with the preliminary discussions and negotiations, and, if unsuccessful, helps find the right litigator.

Litigation attorneys are experts in the process of litigation, including handling court filings, taking depositions, and making court appearances. A litigator would defend you if you are served with a complaint alleging infringement, defamation, breach of contract, or violation of law. Or a litigator would help you assert claims against someone infringing on your work, defaming you, or breaching an agreement.

I advise against hiring a litigator for general business advice. Typically, their orientation is too confrontational.

HOW TO FIND THE RIGHT ATTORNEY

Start by asking people you know for referrals, including members of local writing clubs or self-publishing organizations. Many communities have "lawyers for the arts" groups, which offer discounted or free services to artists. Contact public-interest groups involved in the relevant area, such as organizations promoting fair use or First Amendment rights. You could also contact your local bar association. They often have referral services.

Don't be surprised if you speak to one attorney, who refers you to another attorney, who refers you to yet another attorney. These attorneys are trying to help you find the right person with the right experience and the bandwidth to take you on as a client. Don't assume they are trying to get rid of you.

WHAT TO LOOK FOR IN AN ATTORNEY

Experience, experience, experience, especially in litigation. Nothing is more valuable than an attorney who has handled similar matters for a significant period—ten years at least. An experienced attorney will have a higher hourly rate, but will be able to assess and advise quickly. You are more likely to achieve a better result faster and cheaper.

Responsiveness. This is difficult to measure in first impressions, but try to gauge how quickly the attorney will respond to calls and emails. Ask the attorney about response time.

Chemistry. You must be candid with your attorney, particularly about your mistakes. Are you comfortable talking to this person? Is the attorney a good listener, or dismissive, patronizing, or distracted? Avoid any lawyer who doesn't let you finish your sentences.

Style. Does the attorney seem creative and oriented toward problem-solving? Or a hard-charging bully? Trust me—don't hire a bully. Even if you are really angry or scared, a bully wastes time and money. You will be better off with someone smart, who is fair but tough. Look for an iron fist in a velvet glove.

Warning signs. As I said, avoid bullies. Also avoid gladiators with something to prove to the world. (Not on your nickel, please.) Be wary of attorneys who brag too much about their own achievements or who assure you your case is a "slam dunk." I am suspicious of any attorney who fails to warn clients that litigation is uncertain and expensive in terms of dollars, stress, and distractions. Avoid attorneys with too broad a range of practice areas; that's often a sign of an attorney who will do anything to pay the rent. Check your state bar for any disciplinary actions against the attorney.

Up-front payment. It's fair and appropriate for the attorney to ask for a reasonable retainer, depending on the complexity of the matter. If the payment is high, consider two possibilities. First, the lawyer wants you to understand the expected cost of the matter. You may be gung-ho to sue your former writing partner. By asking for a $20,000 up-front payment or higher, the lawyer is making sure you understand the potential cost of revenge.

Alternatively, the lawyer may not want to handle the matter and hopes you will go away. Ask.

HOW TO HIRE AN ATTORNEY

Organize your information, documents, and thoughts. Be prepared to present the *problem*, and not only your ideas of the solution. I find it difficult to understand a matter when a client calls me and tells me exactly what he wants me to do without explaining the background and his reasons. Often, the proposed solution is off base, and it takes a while to back up the discussion to the underlying problem.

Schedule an initial consultation by phone or in person. Most lawyers will discuss a matter for 15 to 30 minutes without charge or for a flat fee.

Tell the attorney what other parties are involved or potentially involved. If the attorney has a conflict of interest, cut the conversation short.

Be honest. The attorney cannot help you unless all the facts are on the table, especially the embarrassing ones.

Ask for an estimate. The attorney should tell you hourly billing rates and whether a flat fee or contingency fee is possible.

Find out who will be doing the work—the attorney who shakes your hand or a junior associate.

WHAT IF A PROBLEM ARISES?

Here are some of the most common complaints about attorneys:

They fail to communicate and return voicemails and emails. Be realistic. While your legal matter may be the biggest thing in your life, the attorney may be tending many fires. If you leave a message or email and do not hear from the attorney after a few days, leave another message or send a follow-up email. Nudge, but politely. If you do not get an adequate response, consider engaging another attorney.

They overbill or bill above the estimate without warning. Call the attorney and discuss this immediately. Most will discount the bill.

The following are signs of malpractice:

Inattention to the matter. The lawyer should be on top of filing deadlines and respond to communications from the other parties in a timely manner. Failure to do so could harm your case irreparably. If you get any indication your attorney is not on top of your matter, quickly consult with another attorney. If a court-imposed deadline is missed and your case has been compromised, consider filing a malpractice claim.

Failure to account for fees. Even if you prepay fees, you are entitled to receive a detailed bill showing how the fees were applied. If you don't receive one following your request, consider reporting the attorney to the state bar association.

HOW TO CONTROL FEES

Communicate your budget. Be clear about the amount of money you feel comfortable spending. The attorney should let you know whether your budget is reasonable and workable.

Be organized. You are a writer. Present the background, the allegations, and the questions in an easy-to-follow fashion and not in a piecemeal or disjointed manner. If you do not know what information is relevant, err on the side of providing too much. It is faster for the attorney to skim through all the details in order to pick out what's relevant than to identify what's missing and have you fill in the gaps.

Understand what risks you are willing to take. Your attorney could draft a 40-page airtight freelance agreement for your cover designer. But is that really appropriate for a $1,000 contract? Don't pay for a ten-foot cement wall when a picket fence will do.

Engage an attorney with relevant experience. Even if the hourly rate is higher, the cost is likely to be less in the end. And an experienced lawyer will get you through your legal project quickly, so you can get back to writing your next book.

CHAPTER ELEVEN

BEYOND THE BOOK

When my father visited me in college, he often bought me tools: a hammer, drill, screwdriver, ratchet set, vise grip, even a bubble level. When we purchased our home, he gave us a well-equipped toolbox, the most useful gift we ever received.

Consider this book your toolbox for self-publishing. When facing a task that seems daunting, remember CAM. Consider what information you need and what choices will help you do the following:

C	• Control your work
A	• Avoid scams and lawsuits
M	• Maximize tax deductions

With the tools in the *SELF-PUBLISHER'S LEGAL HANDBOOK*, you will control your book by

- owning your own imprint name, ISBNs, domains, cover and interior designs; and banners for your website, Facebook page, Twitter profile, and so on,
- engaging a self-publishing service company with fair and author-friendly business practices,
- setting your own retail price and discount rate,
- owning and controlling your print production files,
- hiring professional editors, designers, and freelancers who assign ownership of the work product to you,
- registering and protecting your copyright and trademarks, and
- understanding the ownership provisions of contracts.

You'll avoid scams, myths, and lawsuits by

- casting a skeptical eye at contests, marketing services, and too-good-to-be-true offers,
- knowing when and how to obtain permissions from copyright owners,
- utilizing public domain, stock images, and low-cost alternatives to expensive copyrighted material,
- operating your website in compliance with laws such as COPPA, DMCA, and CAN-SPAM,
- using show, not tell, to voice your complaints publicly,
- buying the appropriate insurance, and
- hiring the right lawyer at the right time.

And finally, you will maximize tax deductions by

- registering for an EIN and business license,
- obtaining a resale certificate and collecting sales tax,
- separating your business and personal finances,
- maintaining adequate records, and
- running your self-publishing venture as an ongoing business and not as a hobby.

Self-publishing is a new business and still evolving. Law is an old business and still evolving. The tools of this book will undoubtedly need expanding and updating. I am asking for your help.

As a self-published writer, you will see problems and solutions I can't imagine. When you come across egregious contracts, aggressive sales tactics, and fraudulent offers, tell me about them. If you are a victim of DMCA abuse or SLAPP action, spread the word. If you discover time-saving innovations and powerhouse strategies, share the information. Send me emails at info@selfpublisherslegalhandbook.com or leave comments on my blog at http://helensedwick.com/blog/.

The sense of community among self-publishers is extraordinary. On Twitter, Facebook, and on countless blogs, we share tips about writing, character development, formatting, cover design, and platform building. We encourage one another when repeated rejections and basement rankings take their toll. We cheer the self-published author who wins an award or nails a spot on a bestseller list. When we ask for help on forums such as Absolute Write Water Cooler or a Google+ Community, dozens jump in with advice. I cannot think of any other business where so-called competitors share such a strong sense of purpose. We are pioneers together in this business, and together we are changing the publishing world.

ADDENDUM

Understanding Key Contract Provisions

As a self-published author, you are going to be entering into a lot of contracts. For many authors, this is the most uncomfortable task. As I mentioned in the introduction, some of these contracts are so convoluted, they look like 5,000 words run through a blender.

I encourage you to print out the contracts and work through them with a highlighter or pen. If you take the time, you will begin to see patterns and understand the concepts. Below are some hints.

The key provisions to understand are (i) what rights you are granting, (ii) how much control you will have over the publication and sales processes, (iii) how and when you will get paid, (iv) what are your potential liabilities, and (v) how to get out of the contact.

KINDLE DIRECT PUBLISHING TERMS AND CONDITIONS

Contract language	My interpretation
5.5 Grant of Rights. *You grant to each Amazon party,*	Amazon party means Amazon and all their affiliated companies worldwide.

throughout the term of this Agreement	In a later section, the Agreement says that either you or KDP may terminate at any time, so these words are acceptable.
a nonexclusive,	Always look for the word *nonexclusive*. You should not be granting anyone exclusive rights without understanding exactly what you are granting.
irrevocable	Not exactly. You may terminate KDP's right to sell your e-book, but they may continue to support e-books already sold.
right and license to distribute Digital Books,	This is what you want to see—a nonexclusive right for a limited purpose, in this case distributing Digital Books.
directly and through third-party distributors, in all digital formats by all digital distribution means available.	This phrase makes me uncomfortable. Is Amazon going to expand into other formats or become an aggregator like SmashWords? I would not be surprised.
This right includes, without limitation, the right to: *(a) reproduce, index and store Digital Books on one or more computer facilities, and reformat, convert and encode Digital Books;*	These are the rights they need to distribute your e-book. They make sense.

(b) display, market, transmit, distribute, sell and otherwise digitally make available all or any portion of Digital Books through Amazon Properties;	Amazon Properties refers to their website and any other Amazon app or sales channel.
for customers and prospective customers to download, access, copy and paste, print, annotate and/or view online and offline, including on portable devices;	Most of this is fine, but I don't like the copy and paste part.
(c) permit customers to "store" Digital Books that they have purchased from us on servers ("Virtual Storage") and to access and re-download such Digital Books from Virtual Storage from time to time both during and after the term of this Agreement;	This enables readers to move between devices and access their books from the "cloud." Sounds fine to me.
(d) display and distribute (i) your trademarks and logos in the form you provide them to us or within Digital Books (with such modifications as are necessary to optimize their viewing), and (ii) portions of Digital Books, in each case solely for the purposes of marketing, soliciting and selling Digital Books	Good. The license to use any trademark is appropriately limited.
and related Amazon offerings;	I do not know what they mean by related Amazon offerings. Typical Amazon—leaving doors open to new opportunities. The word related works in your favor. The door is not opened too wide.

(e) use, reproduce, adapt, modify, and distribute, as we determine appropriate, in our sole discretion, any metadata that you provide in connection with Digital Books; and	Metadata typically means your name, publication date, and other product information. I wonder what they plan to do with my metadata.
(f) transmit, reproduce and otherwise use (or cause the reformatting, transmission, reproduction, and/or other use of) Digital Books as mere technological incidents to and for the limited purpose of technically enabling the foregoing (e.g., caching to enable display).	Technical mumbo-jumbo.
In addition, you agree that we may permit our affiliates and independent contractors, and our affiliates' independent contractors, to exercise the rights that you grant to us in this Agreement.	While I would prefer to have more control over who else may distribute my e-book, Amazon may only permit others to do what Amazon is permitted to do.
You grant us the rights set forth in this Section 5.5 on a worldwide basis; however, if we make available to you a procedure for indicating that you do not have worldwide distribution rights to a Digital Book, then the territory for the sale of that Digital Book will be those territories for which you indicate, through the procedure we provide to you, that you have distribution rights.	If you do not have worldwide rights to your e-book, you may limit the markets.

3. Term and Termination

We are entitled to terminate this Agreement and your access to your Program account at any time. We will notify you upon termination.

In other provisions, they list reasons why they may terminate, such as your work infringes on someone else's copyright. This right to terminate for no reason is typical, so they do not have to justify their termination. It is acceptable.

You are entitled to terminate at any time by providing us notice of termination, in which event we will cease selling your Digital Books within 5 business days from the date you provide us notice of termination.

This is what you want. The right to terminate at any time without payment of any termination fees.

Following termination, we may fulfill any customer orders for your Digital Books pending as of the date of termination or suspension,

Sounds reasonable.

and we may continue to maintain digital copies of your Digital Books in order to provide continuing access to or re-downloads of your Digital Books or otherwise support customers who have purchased a Digital Book prior to termination or suspension. All rights to Digital Books acquired by customers will survive termination.

All this is reasonable.

5.3.1 *Providing Your List Price.*
You will provide a list price through the KDP website for each Digital Book you submit to us…You may change your List Price through the KDP website, and your change will be effective within 5 business days.

Good. You want to control your list price.

5.3.4 *Customer Prices.*
To the extent not prohibited by applicable laws, we have sole and complete discretion to set the retail customer price at which your Digital Books are sold through the Program.

Amazon may discount the price of your e-book. However, later in the contract they explain that royalty payments are based upon the list price you choose, so their discounting of your e-book will not discount your royalties.

We are solely responsible for processing payments, payment collection, requests for refunds and related customer service, and will have sole ownership and control of all data obtained from customers and prospective customers in connection with the Program.

They will not tell you who bought your e-book. This is typical of Amazon—holding onto information.

5.4.2 *When We Pay You.*
Each Amazon party will pay Royalties due on Digital Book sales approximately 60 days following the end of the calendar month during which the sales were made. At the time of payment, we will make available to you an online report detailing sales of Digital Books and corresponding Royalties.

Nice and clear.

5.4.6 Payment Disputes.
You may not bring a suit or other legal proceeding against us with regard to any statement unless you bring it within six months after the date the statement is available.

Frankly, I don't know how you could contest a payment since you have no access to the underlying sales information. This is a problem even in traditional publishing.

5.8 Representations, Warranties and Indemnities.
You represent and warrant that:
(a) you have the full right, power and authority to enter into and fully perform this Agreement and will comply with the terms of this Agreement;

Among other things, this means that you are at least 18 years old and have the mental capacity to enter into a contract, and you have whatever authority you need from others to grant the licenses and enter into this contract.

(b) prior to you or your designee's delivery of any content, you will have obtained all rights that are necessary for the exercise of the rights granted under this Agreement;

You are assuring them that you have the right to sell your e-book, either because you own the copyright or have obtained all the necessary permissions, licenses, and rights.

(c) neither the exercise of the rights authorized under this Agreement nor any materials embodied in the content nor its sale or distribution as authorized in this Agreement will violate or infringe upon the intellectual property, proprietary or other rights of any person or entity, including, without limitation, contractual rights, copyrights, trademarks, common law rights, rights of publicity, or privacy, or moral rights, or contain defamatory material or violate any laws or regulations of any jurisdiction;	You are responsible if your work is infringing, defamatory, or illegal, so make sure it isn't!
(d) you will ensure that all Digital Books delivered under the Program comply with the technical delivery specifications provided by us; and	Technical requirements are on their website.
(e) you will be solely responsible for accounting and paying any co-owners or co-administrators of any Digital Book or portion thereof any royalties with respect to the uses of the content and their respective shares, if any, of any monies payable under this Agreement.	You promise to pay any co-writers.

To the fullest extent permitted by applicable law, you will indemnify, defend and hold Amazon, its officers, directors, employees, affiliates, subcontractors and assigns harmless from and against any loss, claim, liability, damage, action or cause of action (including reasonable attorneys' fees) that arises from any breach of your representations, warranties or obligations set forth in this Agreement.	This means that if Amazon or anyone else on the list is sued because any of the statements in (a) through (e) are incorrect, or you otherwise breach the contract, you will be obligated to pay the attorneys and all costs and damages for everyone on their list.
We will be entitled, at our expense, to participate in the defense and settlement of the claim or action with counsel of our own choosing.	They will hire their own attorneys, and you will pay their attorneys if you breach the contract.

CREATESPACE SERVICES AGREEMENT.

I have deleted the terms that apply to MP3s and videos.

Contract language	My interpretation
6. Licenses; Ownership; Feedback. **6.1 Content** *Subject to your retained control and ownership of your Content as described in Section 6.4. [6.4 is below.] in order to enable us to provide you with the Services on your behalf, you grant to us a nonexclusive license,*	Good. You want the license to be nonexclusive, so you can use other POD providers as well.
during the term of this Agreement,	In another section, it says either party may terminate at any time.
to...(c) with respect to Books, print, distribute and sell your Book through the CreateSpace E-stores, the Amazon Properties and other sales channels,	This is what you want to see—a nonexclusive license for a limited purpose—printing and selling your books. Nothing more.
You grant us the rights set forth in this Section 6.1 on a worldwide basis; however, if we make available to you a procedure for indicating that you do not have worldwide distribution rights to a Title, then the territory for the sale of that Title will be those territories for which you indicate, through the procedure we provide to you, that you have distribution rights.	Similar to KDP contract.

6.4 Ownership

Subject to the licenses set forth in this Section 6…, and as between the parties, you own all right, title and interest in and to the Content, including all patent, copyright, trademark, service mark, mask work, moral right, trade secret or other intellectual property or proprietary right (collectively, "Intellectual Property Rights") therein.

This is what you want to see. Other than the specific licenses granted, you retain all other rights and ownership in your work.

10. Term; Termination

This Agreement will remain in effect until terminated in accordance with this Section. You may terminate this Agreement at any time by giving notice to us, and we may terminate this Agreement at any time by sending you an e-mail notice at the e-mail address associated with your account. Our notice of such termination will be effective at the time we send you the notice.

Good. You want to be able to terminate at any time.

Upon termination, you will pay us whatever fees were incurred prior to the date of the termination.

CreateSpace provides a number of publishing services. Most likely you will have paid the fees in advance. Some fees are refundable if you are not satisfied. Check their website.

Also upon termination:
  (a) we may fulfill any Customer or-
  ders pending as of the date of termi-
  nation...
	This is reasonable.

Upon termination, we may set off *against any payments to be made to* *you, an amount determined by us to be* *adequate to cover any disputes, charge-* *backs and refunds from your account* *for a prospective three-month period. At* *the end of such three-month period fol-* *lowing termination, we will refund any* *amount not used to offset chargebacks* *and refunds to you, or seek reimburse-* *ment from you via any of the means* *authorized in Section 5.1 above for any* *additional amount required to offset* *chargebacks and refunds, as applicable.*	This gives them the right to hold back any payments to you to cover returns or claims. A three-month holdback period is reasonable.

5.1 Fees
For any Unit sold to a Customer, we
will pay you the applicable Content
License Royalty based on the List Price
of the Unit:
  (a) within 31 days after the end of the
  month in which the Unit sold for
  physical Units sold through the
  CreateSpace E-Stores and the
  Amazon Properties; and
  (b) within 60 days after the end of the
  month in which the Unit is sold for
  physical Units sold through Expanded
  Distribution.
	Timing of payments is clear and reasonable. Like the KDP contract, you set the list price, but CreateSpace/Amazon may discount the retail price. Royalties, however, are based upon the list price you choose. I do not have a problem with that.

7. Representations and Warranties
You acknowledge that we are not the publisher of your Titles (including your Content). You represent and warrant that you will be the publisher of your Titles (including your Content) and, in any case, that you will bear the full and ultimate responsibility for the publication and general distribution of your Titles (including your Content).

By stating that you are the "publisher," CreateSpace is saying you are responsible for the contents of your work; they are merely a printer or "conduit." Being the "publisher" is a short-hand phrase for a bundle or rights and responsibilities. This is acceptable.

You further represent and warrant that
(a) you will comply with all laws, rules, regulations and orders of any governmental authority having jurisdiction over your performance hereunder as applicable in each country (including any local legal requirements with respect to your publication of your Titles, such as making any necessary notifications and filings of copies of your Titles

Consider this a "risk-allocation" provision. Since you cannot say that you **know** your content complies with the laws of every jurisdiction worldwide (there is no way to know that without hiring a team of international lawyers), then you are saying that if it turns out that filings or other steps must be taken in other jurisdictions and countries, you are the one responsible for those filings and actions. This is a risk you are taking and is reasonable.

(b) you have all requisite right, power and authority to enter into this Agreement and perform your obligations hereunder;

This means you are at least 18 years old and have the mental capacity to enter into a contract, and you have whatever authority you need from others to grant the licenses and enter into this contract with CreateSpace. It is reasonable.

(c) prior to your delivery of Content to us you have or have obtained all rights, clearances and permissions to grant the licenses you grant hereunder that are necessary for us to exercise the rights you grant under this Agreement without any further payment obligation by us,...;

You are warranting that you have the right to publish your e-book, either because you own the copyright or have obtained all the necessary permissions, licenses, and rights.

(d) you are granting us the rights, licenses and authorizations you grant hereunder free and clear of any encumbrances, and this Agreement does not violate or conflict with any other arrangements, understandings or agreements between you and any third party;

Encumbrances means liens or other restrictions. Here you are warranting that you will not be violating any other contract by publishing through CreateSpace. For instance, you have not granted to anyone else the exclusive right to publish your book, you are not violating any non-competition or rights of first offer in a traditional publishing contract, and you are not violating any agreement with your co-authors.

(e) the Content (and our use thereof) is not defamatory, libelous, obscene, or otherwise illegal, does not invade any right of privacy, and does not infringe upon any Intellectual Property Right or right of publicity of any person or entity, and any recipe, formula, or instruction contained in the Content is accurate and is not injurious to the user;

Once again, a risk allocation provision. If your book is defamatory or otherwise harmful, you are responsible, not CreateSpace or Amazon.

(f) the Content complies with all aspects of the Content Guidelines as such may be updated from time to time; and

The words Content Guidelines is a link to the page listing these guidelines. This is an example of "incorporation by reference," which means those provisions are made a part of this Agreement. Most online agreements contain multiple links. You should click through to read them.

(g) you are and will be solely responsible for accounting and paying any co-owners or co-administrators of any Content any royalties with respect to the uses of the Content permitted hereunder and their respective shares, if any, of any monies payable hereunder.

You, not CreateSpace, are responsible for paying any co-authors.

8.1 Indemnification

You will indemnify, defend and hold us and our affiliates (and the respective employees, directors, members, managers and representatives of each) and any operator of an Amazon Property harmless from and against any and all claims, judgments, damages and expenses (including without limitation reasonable attorneys' fees) (collectively, "Claims")
(continued on next page)

This means that if Amazon or anyone else on the list is sued because any of your representations or warranties are incorrect or because you breach the contract in any manner, you will be required to pay all attorneys' costs and damages.
(continued on next page)

arising out of any breach or alleged breach by you of the terms of this Agreement, including without limitation the terms contained within the Products and Help pages and the Content Guidelines and Privacy Notice, which are incorporated herein by reference.

Again, the capitalized words are links, another example of incorporating other provisions into this contract. The Help pages alone are endless. This process makes the contract harder to read.

Both the KDP and CreateSpace contracts say that Amazon may change the terms and conditions at any time by posting the changes online, and that your continued use of their services is your agreement to those changes. I do not like these provisions. I used to hope that the courts found them unenforceable, but many courts have upheld them, at least when it comes to the payment of fees. If Amazon tries to expand the scope of its license without providing writers additional notice, I hope courts will not enforce that unilateral expansion.

You will find similar provisions in the terms and conditions of other POD providers and social media sites. You may have no choice but to agree and take your chances.

AN EGREGIOUS CONTRACT

Before you judge Amazon too harshly, take a look at the following provisions from one SPSC's contract. I will not disclose the name because I fear they will come after me. But as of late 2013, the following zingers were in their Terms and Conditions.

Contract language	My interpretation
2. Granting of Rights *The Author transfers to the Publisher without limitation of place the* **exclusive right of reproduction and dissemination** *(Publisher's right) of the work* **for the duration of statutory copyright** *including all additional bibliographical texts and/or images supplied by the Author (e.g., cover text, biographical details) for all print and electronic editions (e-book) and for all print runs without limit of units and in all language versions. In the case of works which have already been published by other publishing houses, a non-exclusive right of use shall be transferred. The Author shall continue to be the copyright holder of his work.*	Translation: If you sign on to this agreement, you are granting the publisher **exclusive** right to publish your book (and all accompanying images and text) in print and electronic formats for the life of the copyright (your life plus 70 years). This is shocking. Don't be fooled by the last sentence, which states that the author continues to be the copyright holder. If you have granted them exclusive right of reproduction and dissemination, then you cannot publish your book elsewhere.
3. Duties and Rights of the Publisher *Design, layout guidelines and delivery dates shall be determined by the Publisher. Sales prices, publishing brand and marketing shall also be determined by the Publisher.*	Remember the concept of controlling your work. You would have no control under this contract.

4. Royalty For each copy (print or e-book) sold and paid for, Author shall receive a royalty of 12% of the average remuneration received by Publisher…Royalties shall be settled every twelve months for the preceding year.

This low royalty rate is more in line with traditional publishing contracts under which you would have received an advance. They pay only once a year.

The contractual parties agree that royalty claims of the Author shall only be disbursed if monthly average royalty claims…exceed 50 Euros (about $68) per month…Author shall, instead of a royalty payment, receive a book voucher to the same value which he may freely redeem for all titles produced by the Publisher.

So if your average monthly royalties (not sales) are less than $68 a month ($816 per year) you get a book voucher and no money. Can it get any worse than this?

BOTTOM LINE

Read and understand your contracts before signing, particularly everything regarding the grant of rights. If you come across an egregious contract, please let me know at

info@selfpublisherslegalhandbook.com.

RESOURCES

BOOKS

Bunnin, Brad and Beren, Peter. *The Writers Legal Companion.* New York: Basic Books, 1998.

Carter, Ruth. *The Legal Side of Blogging: How Not To Get Sued, Fired, Arrested or Killed,* Jents, LLC, 2013.

Crawford, Ted. *Business and Legal Forms for Authors and Self-Publishers.* New York: Allworth Press, 1999.

Duboff, Leonard D. and Krages, Bert P. *Law (In Plain English) for Writers.* Naperville, IL: Sphinx Publishing, 2005.

Galley, Ben; Rooney, Mick; Ross, Orna; Strauss, Victoria. *Choosing a Self-Publishing Service 2013.* London: Font Publications, 2013.

Kawasaki, Guy and Welch, Shawn. *APE; Author, Publisher, Entrepreneur; How To Publish A Book.* Nononina Press, 2013.

Lee, Bonnie, E.A. *Taxpertise: The Complete Book of Dirty Little Secrets.* Irvine, CA: Entrepreneur Press, 2009.

Levine, Mark. *The Fine Print of Self-Publishing.* Minneapolis, MN: Bascom Publishing Group, 2014.

McHale, Robert, Esq. with Gurulay, Eric. *Navigating Social Media Legal Risk: Safeguarding Your Business.* Indianapolis, IN: QUE Publishing, 2012.

Murray, Kay and Crawford, Tad. *The Writer's Legal Guide; Fourth Edition.* New York: Allworth Press, 2013.

Rich, Jason R. *Self-Publishing For Dummies.* Hoboken, NJ: Wiley Publishing, Inc., 2006.

WEBSITES

(Also on my website: http://helensedwick.com/resources/)

- IRS site for obtaining a Federal Employer Identification Number (EIN): http://www.irs.gov/Businesses/Small-Businesses-&-Self-Employed/Apply-for-an-Employer-Identification-Number-%28EIN%29-Online
- Library of Congress Control Number: (http://www.loc.gov/publish/pcn/)
- U.S. Patent and Trademark Office trademark searches: http://tess2.uspto.gov/bin/gate.exe?f=tess&state=4802:rjuqkg.1.1
- General trademark information: http://www.uspto.gov/trademarks/
- R.R. Bowker for buying ISBNs: http://www.isbn.org/
- Bay Area Editors Forum list of editing options: http://www.editorsforum.org/what_do_sub_pages/definitions_copyediting.php
- U.S. Copyright Office Information Circulars: http://www.copyright.gov/circs/

To search for copyright owners:
- http://www.copyright.gov/records/ https://archive.org/details/copyrightrecords.
- Columbia University Libraries: http://copyright.columbia.edu/copyright/permissions/collective-licensing-agencies/#performance-rights
- Google Books: http://books.google.com/googlebooks/copyrightsearch.html
- Stanford University: http://collections.stanford.edu/copyrightrenewals/bin/page?forward=home

- The University of Pennsylvania:
  http://onlinebooks.library.upenn.edu/cce/
- Copyright Clearance Center: http://www.copyright.com/
- Author Registry: http://www.authorsregistry.org/

For international searches:

- The University of Cambridge:
  http://www.caret.cam.ac.uk/copyright/Page48.html

For fine art, graphics and comics:

- Artist Rights Society http://www.arsny.com
- VAGA http://vagarights.com
- Graphics Arts Guide: www.gag.com
- Comicom: www.comicon.com

For songs, lyrics, and sheet music:

- http://www.warnerchappell.com/TemplateAction?system_action=
  getsync_departments&currenttab=licensing
- http://www.alfred.com/Licensing.aspx
- http://www.allmusic.com/genres

Copyright expiration chart from Cornell University:
http://copyright.cornell.edu/resources/publicdomain.cfm

Creative Commons:

- Licenses: http://creativecommons.org/licenses/
- Searches: http://search.creativecommons.org/

Google Images Reverse Searches:
https://www.google.com/imghp?hl=en&tab=wi&ei=T_WHUvOP
KIaajALS10DYAw&ved=0CAQQqi4oAg

Stanford University Fair Use project:
http://cyberlaw.stanford.edu/focus-areas/copyright-and-fair-use.

To identify the owner of an ISP:

- http://www.whois.net/
- http://www.domaintools.com/research/dns/.

Sample takedown notices:

- The National Press Photographers Association site: https://nppa.org/page/5617
- IP Watchdog also provides a sample: http://www.ipwatchdog.com/2009/07/06/sample-dmca-take-down-letter/
- The Electronic Frontier Foundation (EFF) and the Takedown Hall of Shame: https://www.eff.org/takedowns

Federal Trade Commission COPPA rules:

- http://www.business.ftc.gov/documents/Complying-with-COPPA-Frequently-Asked-Questions
- http://www.business.ftc.gov/documents/bus84-childrens-online-privacy-protection-rule-six-step-compliance-plan-your-business
- http://www.business.ftc.gov/documents/alt046-childrens-online-privacy-protection-rule-not-just-kids-sites

Sites for researching the reputation of SPSCs, POD, agents and publishers:

- Absolute Write Water Cooler: http://www.absolutewrite.com/forums/
- Independent Publisher's Magazine: http://www.independentpublisher.com/
- The Independent Publishing Magazine: http://www.theindependentpublishingmagazine.com/
- Predators and Editors: http://pred-ed.com/
- Writer Beware: http://accrispin.blogspot.co.uk/

There are thousands of websites and blogs offering useful advice to writers and self-publishers. In fact, if you search the web, you are risking information overload. Below if a list of my favorite self-publishing blogs and websites, in no particular order. There are countless others.

- Joel Friedlander's The Book Designer:
  http://www.thebookdesigner.com/
- Jane Friedman: http://janefriedman.com/
- Alliance for Independent Authors:
  http://allianceindependentauthors.org/
- Frances Caballo: http://socialmediajustforwriters.com/
- Arlene Miller, The Grammar Diva: http://bigwords101.com/
- Nina Amir: http://ninaamir.com/
- Kimberley Grabas: http://www.yourwriterplatform.com/
- Joanna Penn: http://www.thecreativepenn.com/
- C. S. Larkin: http://www.livewritethrive.com/
- Aaron Shepard Publishing Blog:
  http://www.newselfpublishing.com/blog/
- Duolit: http://selfpublishingteam.com/
- And of course, my blog: http://helensedwick.com/blog/

If this Handbook has been useful for you, please post a review to let others know. Your support and acknowledgement are always greatly appreciated.

ABOUT THE AUTHOR

Helen Sedwick is a California attorney with thirty years of experience representing businesses and entrepreneurs as diverse as wineries, graphic designers, green toy makers, software engineers, restaurateurs, and writers. Her historical novel, *Coyote Winds*, has earned five-star reviews from ForeWord Reviews and Compulsion Reads and is an IndieBRAG Medallion Honoree.

As a small-business owner and published author, she understands the challenges of balancing legal, business, and creative concerns. She wrote the *Self-Publisher's Legal Handbook* to help writers publish and promote their work while minimizing the legal risks.

ACKNOWLEDGEMENTS

I could not have finished this book without the help of talented and dedicated professionals. I want to thank **Mark Chimsky** for his editorial skills and his insights about the publishing world; **Arlene Miller** (the Grammar Diva) for her attention to detail and style; **Ellie Searle** for her clean and polished layout design; **Frances Caballo** for demystifying social media; **Kate McMillan** for creating the website of my dreams; **Joyce Smail** for tax guidance; my friends at **Redwood Writers** for urging me to tackle this project; and **Howard Klepper** for his endless patience, support, and humor.

CPSIA information can be obtained at www.ICGtesting.com
Printed in the USA
LVOW04s1700200415

435320LV00002B/539/P